KNITTING
circles around
MITTENS
and more

creative projects on circular needles

Antje Gillingham

Martingale®
& COMPANY

Knitting Circles around Mittens and More:
Creative Projects on Circular Needles
© 2012 by Antje Gillingham

Martingale & Company®
19021 120th Ave. NE, Suite 102
Bothell, WA 98011 USA
www.martingale-pub.com

Printed in China
17 16 15 14 13 12   8 7 6 5 4 3 2 1

Library of Congress Cataloging-in-Publication Data is available upon request.

ISBN: 978-1-60468-060-7

credits

President & CEO ~ Tom Wierzbicki

Editor in Chief ~ Mary V. Green

Design Director ~ Paula Schlosser

Managing Editor ~ Karen Costello Soltys

Technical Editor ~ Amy Polcyn

Copy Editor ~ Marcy Heffernan

Production Manager ~ Regina Girard

Cover & Text Designer ~ Shelly Garrison

Illustrators ~ Robin Strobel & Ann Marra

Photographer ~ Brent Kane

mission statement

Dedicated to providing quality products
and service to inspire creativity.

dedication

This one's for Ilse Busch, my Oma and the person
who always believed in my abilities!
I continue to love you.

acknowledgments

A huge thank you to Maryann Brown, Laurie
Holmes, Kerma Bowman, and my little daughter,
Katrina, for all their invaluable help and patience in
getting this huge project done.

Thank you to Martingale & Company for their
support and interest in my projects, and for
continuing to publish books with the highest
standards of quality.

contents

introduction

Accessories!

My online resource defines them matter-of-factly as "articles or sets of articles of dress such as gloves, scarves, hats, that add completeness, convenience, attractiveness, etc, to one's basic outfit."

In the early 1900s accessories often took the form of parasols, gloves, hats, and the like. They have left their mark throughout history, sometimes flamboyant, other times modest, but always adding that certain je ne sais quoi to any outfit—the cherry on top of the icing.

Today, accessories are back in the limelight and there's nothing modest about them! Bright color points adorn us during the day; glitz accompanies us at night. Scarves, hats, gloves, and fingerless mitts are worn at any time and in any season.

Accessories are hot! These magical little projects open doors to wispy lace, swaying cables, and creative color play. They beg you to unleash your inner artist and fearlessly conquer even the most involved patterns and techniques. After all, accessories are just small commitments, petite frills to give little fashion kicks to your wardrobe. They are the perfect starting block from which to jump and experiment, learn and practice anything.

"But wait," you interject, "what about the double-pointed needles, those pesky sticks that get caught in the project, my hands, and amongst themselves?" Don't fret, dear knitter. They are no longer the stars of circular knitting but mere extras in the creative process. So keep them in your needle case for now.

This little book will introduce you to the basic techniques of knitting in the round using only two circular needles. The many photos, illustrations, and detailed instructions will allow you to choose your own pace. Work one mitten after the other or try your hand at knitting two at a time! Follow the basic patterns first; then knit embellishments on your circular needle too, such as cables or flowers—you decide!

And while you are liberating yourself from creative as well as technical restraints, let this little gem of a book be the guide on your journey into the fantastic world of knitted accessories.

getting started

Here, you'll find information about the importance of knitting a gauge swatch, as well as how to measure hands and heads to ensure a good fit.

GAUGE

I used to be a very lazy person when it came to knitting a gauge swatch, but a few knitting disasters taught me to knit one before most . . . err, I mean every project. I drill it into my students as well: knit that gauge swatch if you want your stuff to fit. Sometimes I show them what happens when you don't.

The problem is, we want to start that new project with the gorgeous yarn *now*. But, like flossing your teeth, knitting a gauge swatch is tedious yet necessary, especially if you use expensive or substituted yarn or if you work on, say, two mittens simultaneously. It will ensure the correct fit and look of your project. The alternative of ripping out all your hard work is even more painful; believe me, I've been there many times. So bite into that sour apple, knit a swatch, and check those pesky little stitches.

Most patterns tell you to count the stitches over 4". I suggest that my students knit their swatches 6" wide and 6" long. If you try to measure the stitches in a 4" x 4" swatch, they will be distorted and incorrect. Always cast on a few more stitches and knit a little longer to be sure that your gauge is accurate. In the long run it will save you time!

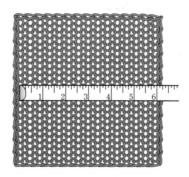

CONVERTING PATTERNS FROM DOUBLE-POINTED TO CIRCULAR NEEDLES

Once you've become comfortable with the basic patterns, you'll be able to convert any pattern from double-pointed needles to two circular needles. Conventional patterns for knitting in the round use either three or four double-pointed needles to set up the project. For clarification, the needles are numbered and carry specific stitches—for example, in the case of mittens, the palm or part of the back of hand stitches. Whatever the case may be, when using two circular needles, the stitches are simply divided in half.

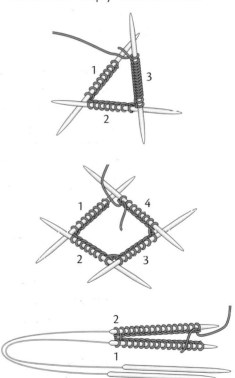

Once you've converted a few patterns, you'll get used to quickly gathering all the necessary information needed from the traditional pattern and transferring it to your circular needles.

MEASURING FOR CORRECT FIT

When measuring for gloves and mittens, measure the dominant hand, because it tends to be a bit larger. Measure the hand circumference around the widest part of the dominant hand, excluding the thumb.

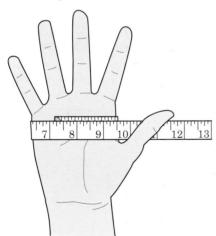

Measure the palm from the top of the wrist to the tip of the middle finger.

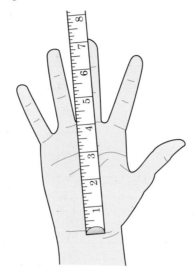

Measure the thumb from where it meets the hand (inside) to its tip.

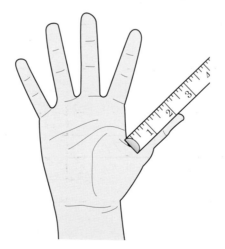

Sizing Tip

If you can't decide between sizes, choose the larger one! Having a little extra room is better than squeezing your hands into mittens that feel too tight.

For hats, measure the head circumference around the widest part of the forehead and back of the head.

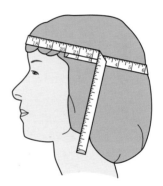

SIZE CHART
Please remember that all measurements are approximate.

Size	Hand Circumference (in inches)	Palm Length (in inches)	Inside Thumb Length (in inches)	Head Circumference (in inches)
Children				
0–6 mos	4	2½	N/A	12½–13
9–18 mos	5	3¾	1¼	13½–14½
2–3 yrs	5½	4¾	1½	15–16
4–6 yrs	6	5½	1¾	16¾
8–10 yrs	6½	6	1¾	17
11–12 yrs	6¾	6½	2	18
13–14 yrs	7	6¾	2	18¾
Women				
Extra Small	6½	6¾	2¼	18¾
Small	6½–6¾	7	2¼	19
Medium	7–7¼	7	2½	20
Large	7½–7¾	7¼	2½	21
Extra Large	8	7¼	2¾	22
Men				
Extra Small	7	7¼	2¾	21
Small	7½–8	7½	2¾	22
Medium	8½–9	7½	3	23
Large	9½–10	7½	3	23½
Extra Large	10½–11	7¾	3¼	23¾
2XL	11½–12	7¾	3¼	24

knitting basics

The following techniques are used to make the projects in this book.

CASTING ON

There are several ways to cast on stitches; here I'll describe some of my favorite methods.

Long-Tail Cast On

I prefer the long-tail cast on because its elasticity is great for cuffs and brims of most any sort. Of course, you can use the one you're familiar with; it may be less confusing and will work just fine.

1. Pull the tail end from the ball of yarn and let a sufficient amount hang down to accommodate the stitches to be cast on. Make a slipknot and slide it onto one of the needles. The tail end should face you. Hold the needle in your right hand.

    Squeeze your left thumb and index finger together and spread the remaining three fingers straight out. Slip your thumb and index finger (still squeezed together) between the two strands of yarn so that the tail hangs over your thumb and the working yarn hangs

over your index finger. Grab the two strands of yarn, which are lying across your palm, with the remaining three fingers and open the thumb and index finger to look like an imaginary gun. Make sure the palm of the left hand faces you and the needle tip points toward the thumb.

2. Move the needle toward you and all the way down until it reaches the base of the thumb. Slide the needle under the outside strand of yarn wrapped around the thumb and up through the loop in front of the thumb.

3. Now move the needle over and behind the strand of yarn wrapped around the index finger and scoop it up. Then guide the needle from the top back into the loop in front of the thumb, down, and toward you. Let the thumb slip from under the yarn strand and gently pull the front strand down to tighten the stitch on the needle. Remember, you don't want the stitches too tight around the needle. Instead,

they should be slightly loose with space left for you to start knitting the first round.

Repeat steps 2 and 3 until the desired number of stitches have been cast on.

To ball of yarn

To cut end

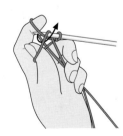

Cable Cast On

Begin by making a slipknot and sliding it onto a needle. Hold the needle in your left hand. Pick up the empty needle with your right hand and insert it into the slipknot knitwise; wrap the working yarn around the needle and pull the needle back out of the stitch as if to knit, but don't pull the old stitch off the left needle. Instead transfer the new stitch from the right to the left needle, sliding it in front of the slipknot.

*Next, insert the right needle between the two stitches on the left needle. Wrap the yarn around it and pull the needle back out as if to knit and slide it to the left needle without pulling the old stitches off. Repeat from * until the desired number of stitches have been cast on.

Backward Loop Cast On

Begin by making a slipknot and sliding it onto a needle. Hold the needle in your right hand and wrap the working yarn around your left thumb as illustrated.

*Slide the needle under the strand section wrapped around the side of the thumb closest to you. Then slip it over the opposite section, close to your index finger. Scoop the strand up and toward you. There are two stitches on the right-hand needle. Repeat from * until the desired number of stitches have been cast on.

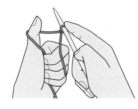

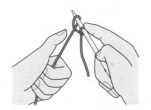

Provisional Cast On

I am not very good at crocheting; so when the instructions tell me to chain a certain amount of stitches, and then knit into their back loops for the provisional cast on, I usually have to scream! Where are those back loops? I certainly can't see them. Here is a method that works great even for the non-crocheter.

You'll need waste yarn, a straight needle one size bigger than the pattern asks for, and a crochet hook that somewhat matches the knitting needle in size.

Make a slipknot and slide it onto the hook. Hold the hook in your right hand and the knitting needle and working yarn in your left hand, making sure that the yarn is behind the knitting needle.

Guide the hook across the front of the needle and scoop up the working yarn from underneath.

Gently pull the working yarn through the stitch on the hook. This may take a little practice but works wonderfully in the long run!

Continue to cast on in this manner until the required number of stitches are on the left-hand needle. Scoop up and slip the yarn directly through the stitch on the hook several times before cutting the yarn and securing the loop (this last action is called "chaining").

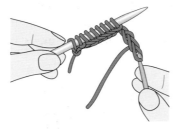

DECREASES

There are several different ways to work decreases. Depending on where they occur in the project, they have to slant this way or that to make the whole look marvelous.

Right-Slanting Decreases

Knit two together (K2tog). Insert the needle into the next two stitches knitwise and knit them together as if they were one stitch. You've decreased one stitch.

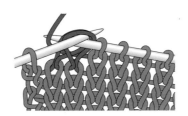

Purl two together (P2tog). Insert the needle into the next two stitches purlwise and purl them together as if they were one stitch. You've decreased one stitch.

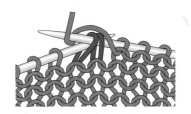

Left-Slanting Decreases

Slip, slip, knit (ssk). Slip one stitch as if to knit; then slip the next stitch as if to knit. Insert the left-hand needle through the front of both stitches, but don't slip them back.

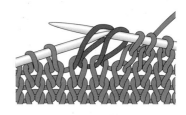

The right-hand needle is now sitting behind the left-hand needle. Use the right-hand needle to knit the two stitches together through the back loops. You've decreased one stitch.

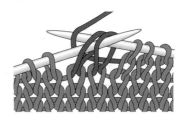

INCREASES

Increases can be made using a variety of techniques, depending on the desired look. Some are subtle in appearance, while others, such as K1f&b, are more prominent.

Make 1 (M1)

This book uses two variations of the "make one" stitch (M1). If the pattern doesn't indicate which one to work, use the one you are most comfortable with.

Make one stitch right (M1R). Slip the left-hand needle under the horizontal bar located between two stitches, from back to front. Notice how this "new" stitch is twisted. With the right-hand needle, knit into the front as with any other stitch. You've increased one stitch.

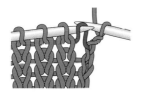

Insert left needle from back to front under horizontal bar.

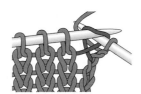

Knit into front of stitch.

Make one stitch left (M1L). Slip the left-hand needle under the horizontal bar located between two stitches, from front to back. Notice how this "new" stitch is twisted. With the right-hand needle, knit through the back loop of this stitch. You've increased one stitch.

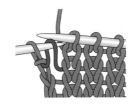

Insert left needle from front to back through "running thread."

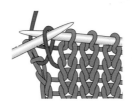

Knit into back of stitch.

Lifted Increase Right (LIR)

Knit into the "shoulder" (not center) of the stitch below by inserting the right-hand needle immediately behind the stitch on the left-hand needle and into only the very top of the stitch below. Then knit the stitch on the left-hand needle as you normally would. You've increased one stitch.

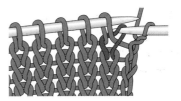

Lifted Increase Left (LIL)

Insert the left-hand needle immediately behind the stitch just worked and into the "shoulder" only (not center) of the stitch below and knit. You've increased one stitch.

Knit into Front and Back of Stitch (K1f&b)

Insert the right-hand needle into the stitch, wrap the yarn around the needle, and pull it back out toward you as if to knit. Do not pull the old stitch off the left-hand needle. Instead, insert the right-hand needle into the back loop of the same stitch, wrap the yarn around the needle and pull it up and back out. You've increased one stitch.

Knit into stitch but do not drop it off left needle.

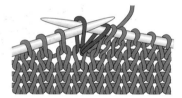

Knit into back of same stitch.

I-CORD

In order to work an I-cord, you can use either a circular needle or double-pointed needles of the appropriate size. The right side of the cord will always face you.

Knit one row, but do not turn. *Slide all the stitches to the opposite end of the needle. Notice that the working yarn is now hanging away from the needle tip. Pull the working yarn behind your project to the tip and knit across all stitches. Repeat from * until the cord measures the desired length; then bind off.

DUPLICATE STITCH (SWISS DARNING STITCH)

The duplicate stitch is an easy method to embroider knitted fabric and is worked from a chart. It can be used in lieu of intarsia (color block or picture knitting) on flat pieces and also on garments worked in the round.

Decide where you want to place your design, and thread a tapestry needle with the same-weight yarn as used for the project. Work with yarn strands about 15" to 20" long to avoid tangling or breaking.

Horizontal Stitches

The horizontal duplicate stitch is worked from right to left; begin work in the lower right-hand corner of the image. Bring the needle from the wrong side to the right side of the fabric through the center of the stitch below the V point of the first stitch to be duplicated. Pull the yarn through to the front, leaving a tail on the wrong side.

*Pass the needle from right to left under both legs of the V point of the stitch right above the stitch to be duplicated. Gently pull the strand to the left, easing it onto half of the knitted stitch to be covered.

Reinsert the needle below the V point of the stitch to be duplicated, from the right side to the wrong side. Then bring it back up to the right side through the middle of the stitch on the left below the V point of the next stitch to be duplicated.

Bring the needle up through the base of the stitch to the left of the stitch just duplicated.

Repeat from * as needed.

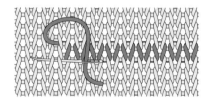

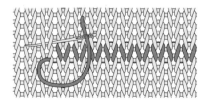

Vertical Stitches

The vertical stitch is worked the same as the horizontal stitch; only here you start at the lowest point of your motif and work upward, and instead of finishing the stitch to the left, the needle comes up to the right side through the center of the stitch above the last duplicated stitch.

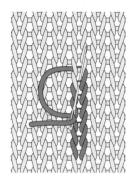

FAIR ISLE

Fair Isle or stranded knitting is the technique used when working with multiple yarns in a row or round. It uses two or more strands of different-colored yarns to create a multitude of designs and patterns. There are different ways to work a Fair Isle pattern.

Drop and pick up each color as you use it. This is the simplest and probably the slowest method to get your Fair Isle on. Begin knitting with the main color (A), and when it's time to change to the contrasting color (B), drop A and attach B as if you're starting a new ball of yarn. Knit with B as per pattern, and then drop it and grab A as needed.

Guide A *underneath* B and continue to knit. When it's time to change color again, drop A, pick B and guide it *over* A. Alternate the colors in this manner, always running A under and B over the "resting" strand of color.

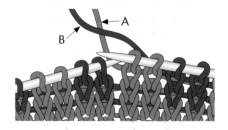

Hold one strand of color in your left hand and one strand in your right hand, thus working with both colors at the same time.

Once conquered, this is one of the fastest and smoothest ways to work Fair Isle. The magic word is practice . . . practice and practice! For this technique, hold A in the hand you normally hold your yarn, and B in the other hand. Begin to knit using each color strand/hand as needed. The strand from your right hand will always lie above the strand from your left hand. Take your time to work with both hands and try not to pull the yarn too tightly—the fabric will pucker. If you work too loosely, the strand of the other color will show through. Simply go down a needle size and try again.

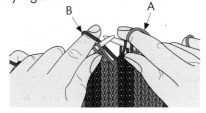

A is held with the right hand,
B with the left hand.

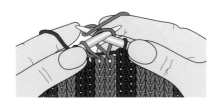

Work first A stitch with
"throwing" method.

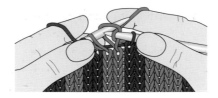

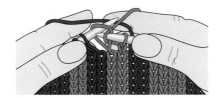

Work second A stitch the same way.

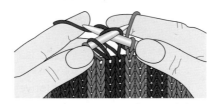

Work first B stitch with "picking" method.

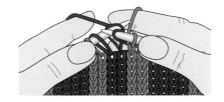

Continue working B with "picking" method
and A with "throwing" method.

SEAMING

Following are the two seaming methods used for the projects in this book.

Three-Needle Bind Off

With the right sides of the work facing each other (wrong sides are facing outward), and with the needle tips parallel and facing to the right, hold both needles in your left hand.

The yarn tail hangs on the right side of your work and one needle sits in front of the other. Use a third *larger-sized* knitting needle as needed for this bind off.

Pass the larger needle in your right hand through the first stitch on each left-hand needle; knit them together. *Knit the next stitch on both left-hand needles together. There are two stitches on the right needle; bind off one stitch as you would for the traditional bind off;

repeat from * until all the stitches have been bound off.

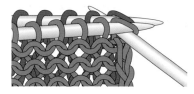

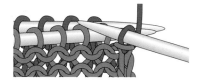

Kitchener Stitch (Grafting)

Many knitters seem to be afraid of the Kitchener stitch. While we may not quite understand it, its effect on a seam is simply amazing.

Hold the pieces to be joined in your left hand, with right sides facing outward. The yarn tail hangs on the right side of the work and one needle sits in front of the other. Thread the yarn onto the tapestry needle. As you weave the yarn through the stitches, make sure you pass it under the needles, back and forth at all times.

When starting the Kitchener stitch in the traditional manner (work the first stitch on the front needle purlwise and work the first stitch on the back needle knitwise), I noticed a little "ear" in the corner. One day I started the process as described in step 1 and saw that there was no little ear. So you can choose whether to start in the traditional way or try my way.

1. Weave the yarn through the first stitch on the front needle knitwise and push the stitch off the needle. Then weave the yarn through the next stitch on the front needle purlwise (now the first stitch) and leave it on the needle. Gently pull the yarn to match the tension of the rest of the knitted fabric. Weave the yarn through the first stitch on the back needle purlwise and push the stitch off the needle. Again, pull the yarn gently to keep the tension even as the seam closes up. Then weave the yarn through the next stitch on the back needle knitwise (now the first stitch) and leave it on the needle.

2. Weave the yarn through the first stitch on the front needle knitwise and push that stitch off the needle. Weave the yarn through the next stitch (now the first stitch) on the front needle purlwise and leave it on the needle.

3. Weave the yarn through the first stitch on the back needle purlwise and push the stitch off the needle. Weave the yarn through the next stitch (now the first stitch) on the back needle knitwise and leave it on the needle.

Repeat steps 2 and 3 until there are two stitches left, one in front and one in back. Weave the yarn through the first stitch on the front needle knitwise, and then push that stitch off the needle. Weave the yarn through the first stitch on the back needle purlwise and push it off the needle. Pull the tapestry needle and yarn through to the wrong side and weave in the tail.

Here's the shorthand version of grafting.

Begin with:

Front knit off, purl on

Back purl off, knit on

Continue with:

Front knit off, purl on

Back purl off, knit on

End with:

Front knit off

Back purl off

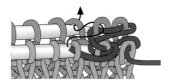

Front knit off, purl on.
Back purl off, knit on.

Front knit off, purl on.

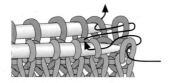

Back purl off, knit on.

CLOSING THE GUSSET GAP

In her book *Sensational Knitted Socks* (Martingale & Company, 2005), Charlene Schurch shows a wonderful way to avoid the hated gap or hole that often occurs when picking up stitches for the heel gusset on a sock. This pitfall doesn't only plague sock knitters. Make way for the thumb gusset!

I've modified Charlene's trick a little to suit my knitting needs and it works perfectly.

Look closely at the gusset corner and find the last horizontal bar that connects thumb gusset with the thumb cast-on edge. To close the gap, pick up both stitches by inserting your knitting needle into the thumb-gusset stitch from front to back, and then into the thumb cast-on edge stitch from back to front. You now have both stitches sitting on your right-hand needle. Knit them together to close the notorious gap!

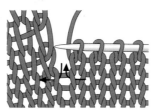

Picking up stitches
when both were knit

KNOTS AND TAILS

When working on your project, you may encounter an irregularity or even a knot in your yarn. This seems to hold true especially for hand-dyed yarns.

I highly recommend that you cut before and restart the yarn beyond the problem area, leaving tails on both the end of the old and the beginning of the new strand. These tails will be woven in later. If you decide to continue and knit the faulty yarn, it could very well open and unravel later. Once this happens, there are no tails to fix the weak spot and all your hard work will go into the trash.

To weave in the tails, slip the tapestry needle through the yarn strands, actually splitting them (rather than the traditional way of going under and over the yarn strands) in a wavelike manner. This makes the tail invisible from the right side of the fabric. You can weave in horizontally, vertically, or diagonally—whichever you prefer.

SLIPPING STITCHES

When I teach my workshops, a lot of students ask me which way to slip the stitches from one needle to the other. When you read a pattern and it instructs you to slip one or more stitches without specifying whether to do so as if to knit or as if to purl, you are expected to slip your stitches as if to purl. Unless your pattern tells you specifically to slip the stitches knitwise, you'll *always* slip them purlwise.

TIGHTENING STITCHES AT THE BEGINNING OF A ROUND

In order to tighten the working yarn at the beginning of each set of stitches, try this: knit the first two stitches in the pattern, and then pause to pull the strand really tight before continuing the row. After knitting the first few rounds, it may seem that no matter how tight you pull your yarn, a slight gap remains at each turn. It will disappear completely as long as

you remember to continue to knit the first two stitches, and then pull the strand tightly every time. Should the closing of the round remain uneven, you can always ease it into shape as you weave in your tail at the end.

UNDERSTANDING ROWS AND ROUNDS

For many of my students, the hardest question to answer when knitting in the round on two circular needles is: Is it a row or is it a round? Well, it's both. Take a look at your work. There are two separate projects on your needles, as in the "Basic Fingerless Mittens" pattern (page 20). Each mitten in turn is divided into two halves; one of which sits on the 24" needle and the other sits on the 16" needle. When you begin to knit, you'll work the two halves on one needle, which is a row. When you get to the end of one needle, you turn your work (this is one half of the round) and knit the other two halves of your mittens as in a row.

Then you'll turn your work again, thus completing two rows, which equals one complete round.

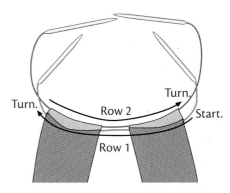

Unless otherwise specified, the pattern will list rounds only, and each round consists of two rows (16" and 24" needles). For example, you may see this instruction given for round 1:

Rnd 1: Knit.

This means that you work the rows as follows:

Row 1 (16" needle): **Right mitten (RM):** Knit. Rep for left mitten **(LM)**. Turn.

Row 2 (24" needle): **LM:** Knit. Rep for **RM**. Turn.

basic fingerless mittens

These basic fingerless mittens are the perfect project for you to sneak a peek into the world of knitting accessories two at a time. But be forewarned! These innocent little coverings will wrap their threads around you, fiber by fiber, and gradually you'll feel compelled to provide warmth and comfort to, well . . . everyone!

Skill level: Easy ◧◼◻◻

Sizes: Women's Small (Medium, Large)

To fit hand circumference up to: 6¾ (7¼, 7¾)"

MATERIALS

1 (1, 2) balls of Tonalita from Trendsetter Yarns (52% wool, 48% acrylic; 1.75 oz/50 g; 100 yds/91 m) in color 2376 Rio 🌀4

2 size 6 (4 mm) circular needles (16" and 24") or size required to obtain gauge

Point protectors

2 regular and 2 lockable stitch markers

Tapestry needle

Small amount of waste yarn

GAUGE

5½ sts = 1" in St st

Avoiding Tangles

If using only one ball of yarn, wind it into two, rather than trying to knit from both ends. Otherwise, the strands will become horribly tangled and make learning this method very confusing and frustrating.

SETTING UP THE NEEDLES

1. CO 32 (32, 36) sts for your first mitten, using 1 of your 2 balls of yarn and the 16" needle.

2. Sl 16 (16, 20) sts pw from 16" needle to 24" needle. The working strand of yarn (the one attached to your ball) as well as the open end of your CO edge should now face away from the needle tips and toward the cables.

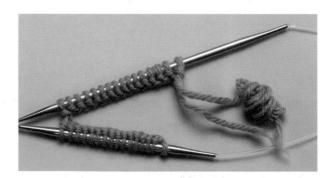

3. Push all sts simultaneously to the other end of both needles. The working yarn should now hang from the tip of your 24" needle, and the open side of your CO edge should face the needle tips.

4. Make sure sts aren't twisted and CO edge faces neatly inward. Thread the tail onto a tapestry needle and weave it through first st on opposite side as shown. Using tail and working yarn, tie a tight double knot to close rnd of first mitten.

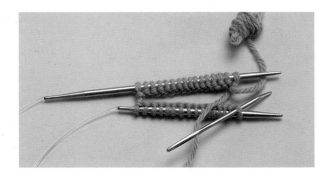

5. Slide first mitten sts closer to cables or put point protectors on tips and ignore it for now. For second mitten, use ball 2 of yarn. Using the 16" needle, CO 32 (32, 36) sts on empty end of your circular needle so your work looks like that shown above right.

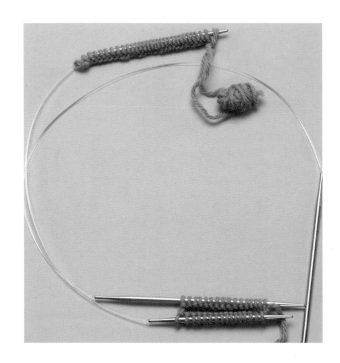

6. Using empty 24" needle tip, sl 16 (16, 20) sts pw onto it. The working yarn as well as the open end of second CO edge should both face away from the needle tips and toward the cables.

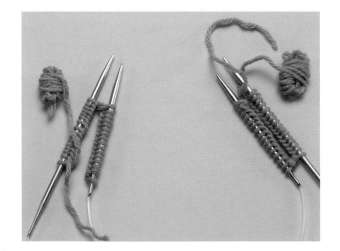

7. As before, slip tail onto tapestry needle and, after making sure your sts are not twisted and the CO edge is facing inward, thread it through the first st of the opposite side. Using the working yarn and the tail, tie a tight double knot to close the gap. Scoot second mitten along the cables toward first mitten.

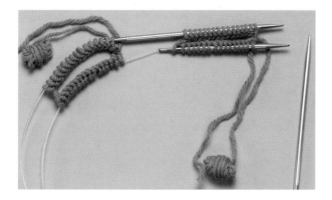

If you're running out of time or need to clear your head, this is a great stopping point. It's best to put the mittens down and come back to them later if you're unfocused or feeling rushed.

PREPARING TO KNIT

Let's knit the first row (half a rnd) step by step. Before you beg, notice that needles are parallel and tips face away from each other. Place point protectors on each end of 24" needle because you'll be knitting on 16" needle first. The 16" needle (row 1) is beg of rnd. If you need help remembering, place a marker between the first and second stitches on needle to indicate beginning of rnd. First mitten on 16" needle is right mitten (RM), and second mitten is the left mitten (LM).

1. Scoot sts of RM close to needle tips and let LM rest on cables. Holding needles in your left hand (LH) with working yarn at tips, make sure 24" needle sits *slightly behind* 16" needle. Working yarn hangs between both needles for RM. Strand of yarn for LM should lie over and behind cable of 24" needle. This way it will already be set up for later use without getting tangled or accidentally creating an extra st.

2. Pull the end of 24" needle to right and down so that sts on it slide onto its cable. With your right hand (RH), pick up empty end of 16" needle and get ready to knit your first row. Make sure you squeeze tip of 16" needle and cable of 24" needle tightly tog; this will prevent a gap from forming.

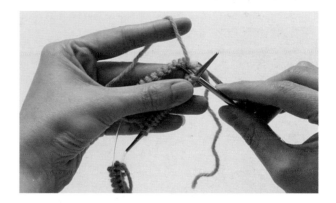

CUFF

Beg with 16 (16, 16) sts of RM: K1, pm (optional), K1, P2, *K2, P2; rep from * to end. If you placed the stitch marker, it indicates beg of rnd from now on. Notice how needle position has changed after you've finished ribbing first 16 (16, 16) sts. The 16" needle is no longer parallel to 24" needle; tips are now facing each other. This is an excellent and important reminder that you still have not completed the row and that you still have to work 16 (16, 16) sts of cuff for LM.

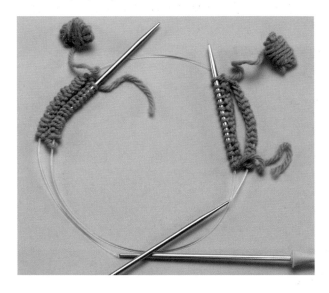

Slide sts of RM to right toward cable and away from needle tip; let it rest. Make sure working yarn hangs behind 16" needle as well as over and behind cable of 24" needle. Scoot sts of LM close to needle tip, making sure working yarn is picked up from between cable of 24" needle and tip of 16" needle, and doesn't create an extra st.

Again, squeeze needle tip and cable together to avoid creating a gap. Once more, work in K2, P2 ribbing for cuff.

You've now completed 1 row or first half of a rnd for your mittens. Notice how needles have opened up and lie parallel once again. Looking at your work, you'll see you've worked half of each cuff.

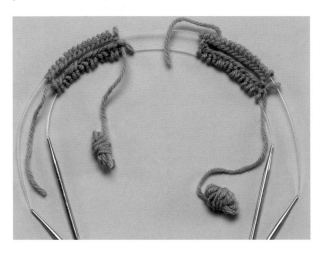

To start second row of first rnd, turn work so that unribbed sts of CO edge face you and needle tips with working yarn attached are in your LH. This time you'll knit off the 24" needle, so switch point protectors to tips of 16" needle. Remember to switch balls as you switch mittens and make sure working strand of yarn hangs between the two needles and resting strand of yarn lies over and behind back cable.

Align tips and hold 16" needle *slightly behind* 24" needle. As before, pull back needle (16") to right and down so its sts slip onto cable. Squeeze needle tip (24") and cable (16") close tog and start ribbing.

Notice how tips of the 24" needle face each other after you've worked cuff for LM. Remember that you're only done with half of this row. You still have to knit cuff for RM to finish row completely. Once needles are parallel again, you should be ready to start first row of second rnd at st marker.

You've finished a complete rnd for your mittens and your needles are once again parallel.

Work even in K2, P2 ribbing using previous guidelines until cuff measures 2 (2, 2¼)" or desired length. The repetitions will help you to quickly get the hang of this technique. Remember to switch point protectors onto tips of resting needle. It will help you get used to using the correct needle to knit. Soon you'll feel confident enough and won't need them anymore.

With sts on 16" needle facing, hook a lockable marker to RM cuff to help remember which mitten is which as you knit.

BODY

Rnd 1 (inc rnd):

Small

Row 1 (16" needle): **RM:** K1, M1R, knit to last st, M1R, K1. Rep for **LM**. Turn. (18 sts per half)

Row 2 (24" needle): Knit. Turn.

Medium

Row 1 (16" needle): **RM:** K1, M1R, knit to last st, M1R, K1. Rep for **LM**. Turn. (18 sts per half)

Row 2 (24" needle): **LM:** K1, M1R, knit to last st, M1R, K1. Rep for **RM**. Turn. (18 sts per half)

Large

Row 1 (16" needle): **RM:** K1, M1R, knit to last st, M1R, K1. Rep for **LM**. Turn. (18 sts per half)

Row 2 (24" needle): Knit. Turn.

All Sizes

[34 (36, 38) sts total per mitten.]

Rnds 2–7: Knit.

THUMB GUSSET

All Sizes

Rnd 1:

Row 1: **RM:** K1f&b, K1, K1f&b, knit to end. Rep for **LM**. Turn. (20 sts per half)

Row 2: Knit. Turn.

Rnds 2 and 3: Knit.

Rnd 4:

Row 1: **RM:** K1f&b, K3, K1f&b, knit to end. Rep for **LM**. Turn. (22 sts per half)

Row 2: Knit. Turn.

Rnds 5 and 6: Knit.

Rnd 7:

Row 1: RM: K1f&b, K5, K1f&b, knit to end. Rep for **LM**. Turn. (24 sts per half)

Row 2: Knit. Turn.

Rnds 8 and 9: Knit.

Rnd 10:

Row 1: RM: K1f&b, K7, K1f&b, knit to end. Rep for **LM**. Turn. (26 sts per half)

Row 2: Knit. Turn.

Rnds 11 and 12: Knit.

Rnd 13:

Row 1: RM: K1f&b, K9, K1f&b, knit to end. Rep for **LM**. Turn. (28 sts per half)

Row 2: Knit. Turn.

Rnds 14 and 15: Knit.

Large

Rnd 16:

Row 1: RM: K1f&b, K11, K1f&b, knit to end. Rep for **LM**. Turn. (30 sts per half)

Row 2: Knit. Turn.

Rnds 17 and 18: Knit.

All Sizes

Next rnd:

Row 1: RM: Sl 13 (13, 15) sts to waste yarn. Using backward loop cast on (page 11), CO 3 sts to RH needle tip, knit to end. Rep for **LM**. Turn.

Row 2: Knit. Turn. [34 (36, 38) sts total per mitten]

Mittens should now measure approx 5 (5, 5½)" from CO edge. Knit even until mittens measure approx 6¾ (7, 7¼)" or 1" less than desired length from CO edge.

Work in K1, P1 ribbing for 1"; then BO all sts in pattern as follows:

Row 1: RM: BO, to last st and put it on lockable marker. Rep for **LM**. Turn.

Row 2: Sl st from marker to RH needle, cont to BO rem sts for **LM**. Rep for **RM**. Turn.

THUMB

Setup

RM: With thumb gusset on right, sl 6 (6, 7) sts from waste yarn to 16" needle, beg at thumb gusset and working toward mitten body. Cont with same needle tip and rep for **LM**. Turn.

LM: With thumb gusset on left, sl rem 7 (7, 8) sts from waste yarn to 24" needle. Cont with same needle tip and rep for **RM**. Turn.

[13 (13, 15) sts total per thumb]

Connect the two mittens with a piece of scrap yarn or a lockable marker right above the cuff to keep them close together as you work. Make sure to slip mittens behind needle cables and out of the way each time you turn your work.

Rnd 1:

Row 1 (16" needle): RM: Reattach yarn, K6 (6, 7), PU 3 sts in CO edge (see picking up thumb-gusset sts on page 18). Rep for **LM**. [9 (9, 10) sts per half]

Sl mittens behind both cables.

Row 2 (24" needle): LM: With RH needle tip, PU 1 st in CO edge, K7 (7, 8). Rep for **RM**. Turn. [8 (8, 9) sts per half]

[17 (17, 19) sts total per thumb]

Next 5 rnds: Knit.

Next rnd:

Row 1: RM: *K1, P1; rep from * to last 1 (1, 0) st, K1f&b (K1f&b, K0). Rep for **LM**. Turn. (10 sts per half)

Row 2: LM: *K1, P1; rep from * to last 0 (0, 1) st, K0 (0, K1f&b). Rep for **RM**. Turn. [8 (8, 10) sts per half]

Cont in K1, P1 ribbing for 3 more rnds or until desired length. BO in patt.

Weave in ends.

bella donna

Bella Donna possesses an understated elegance and a difficulty level you control. Work up the basic pattern, and then choose whether or not to attach the cable belt or flower, or both. I used one of my favorite yarns, Shepherd Worsted from Lorna's Laces. It knits up beautifully and soft, and it looks gorgeous on its own should you decide to stay with the simple chic of a fluted cuff.

Skill level: Easy ◼◼☐☐

Sizes: Women's Small (Medium, Large)

To fit hand circumference up to: 6¾ (7¼, 7¾)"

MATERIALS

A 1 skein of Shepherd Worsted from Lorna's Laces (100% superwash merino wool; 3.5 oz/100 g; 225 yds/206 m) in color 7ns Cedar ④

B 15 yds Angora from Prism Yarns (100% French angora; 1 oz/28 g; 90 yds/82 m) in color Lipstick

2 size 4 (3.5 mm) circular needles (16" and 24") or size required to obtain gauge

2 size 7 (4.5 mm) straight needles

Small amount of embroidery thread

18 size 6/0 glass beads

Beading needle

Cable needle

5 lockable stitch markers

Point protectors

Tapestry needle

Small amount of waste yarn

GAUGE

5 sts = 1" in St st

SPECIAL INSTRUCTIONS

4/4 RC: Sl 4 sts to cn and hold in back, K4, K4 from cn.

CUFF

With smaller circular needles and A, CO and set up 80 sts (40 sts per half) per mitten. Follow instructions for "Setting Up the Needles" (page 20).

Rnds 1 and 2: *K4, P4; rep from * to end.

Rnd 3: *K4, P1, P2tog, P1; rep from * to end. (70 sts total per mitten)

Rnd 4: *K4, P3; rep from * to end.

Rnd 5: *K4, P2tog, P1; rep from * to end. (60 sts total per mitten)

Rnd 6: *K4, P2; rep from * to end.

Rnd 7: *K4, P2tog; rep from * to end. (50 sts total per mitten)

Rnd 8: *K4, P1; rep from * to end.

Rnd 9: *K2tog, K2, P1; rep from * to end. (40 sts total per mitten)

Rnd 10: *K3, P1; rep from * to end.

Small

Dec rnd: *P1, P2tog, (P6, P2tog) twice, P1; rep from * to end. (34 sts total per mitten)

Medium

Dec rnd: *P1, P2tog, purl to last 3 sts, P2tog, P1; rep from * to end. (36 sts total per mitten)

Large

Dec rnd:

Row 1: RM: P1, P2tog, purl to end. Rep for **LM**. Turn.

Row 2: LM: P1, P2tog, purl to end. Rep for **RM**. Turn. (38 sts total per mitten)

All Sizes

Work in K1, P1 ribbing until cuff measures approx 2¼ (2½, 2½)" from CO edge.

> #### Note
> Sizes Small and Large will begin and end with K1 on the 16" needle, and with P1 on the 24" needle, while Medium begins with K1 and ends with P1 on both needles.

BODY

Next rnd: Knit.

Place 2 lockable markers in each mitten for cable-band placement as follows:

RM: On 24" needle directly under thumb gusset, place one marker in last st of first ribbed row, and one in last st on LH needle.

LM: On 16" needle directly under thumb gusset, place one marker in first st of first ribbed row, and one in first st on LH needle.

Knit even for 4 (5, 6) rnds.

THUMB GUSSET

Rnd 1:

Row 1: RM: K1, M1R, K1, M1L, knit to end. Rep for **LM**. Turn. [19 (20, 21) sts per half]

Row 2: Knit. Turn.

Rnds 2 and 3: Knit.

Rnd 4:

Row 1: RM: K1, M1R, K3, M1L, knit to end. Rep for **LM**. Turn. [21 (22, 23) sts per half]

Row 2: Knit. Turn.

Rnds 5 and 6: Knit.

Rnd 7:

Row 1: RM: K1, M1R, K5, M1L, knit to end. Rep for **LM**. Turn. [23 (24, 25) sts per half]

Row 2: Knit. Turn.

Rnds 8 and 9: Knit.

Rnd 10:

Row 1: RM: K1, M1R, K7, M1L, knit to end. Rep for **LM**. Turn. [25 (26, 27) sts per half]

Row 2: Knit. Turn.

Rnds 11 and 12: Knit.

Rnd 13:

Row 1: RM: K1, M1R, K9, M1L, knit to end. Rep for **LM**. Turn. [27 (28, 29) sts per half]

Row 2: Knit. Turn.

Rnds 14 and 15: Knit.

Large

Rnd 16:

Row 1: RM: K1, M1R, K11, M1L, knit to end. Rep for **LM**. Turn. (31 sts per half)

Row 2: Knit. Turn.

Rnds 17 and 18: Knit.

All Sizes

Next rnd:

Row 1: **RM:** Sl 13 (13, 15) sts to waste yarn and using backward loop cast on (page 11), CO 3 sts to RH needle tip. Knit to end. Rep for **LM**. Turn.

Row 2: Knit. [34 (36, 38) sts total per mitten]

Mittens measure approx 4¾ (5, 5½)" from CO edge. Knit even until mittens measure 6½ (7, 7¼)" or 1" less than desired length from CO edge.

Work in K1, P1 ribbing for 1"; then BO as for "Basic Fingerless Mittens" (page 27).

THUMB
Setup

RM: With thumb gusset on right, sl 6 (6, 7) sts from waste yarn to 16" needle, beg at thumb gusset and working toward mitten body. Cont with same needle tip and rep for **LM**. Turn.

LM: With thumb gusset on left, sl rem 7 (7, 8) sts from waste yarn to 24" needle. Cont with same needle tip and rep for **RM**. Turn.

[13 (13, 15) sts total per thumb]

Connect the two mittens with a piece of scrap yarn or a lockable marker right above the cuff to keep them close together as you work. Make sure to slip mittens behind needle cables and out of the way each time you turn your work.

Rnd 1:

Row 1 (16" needle): RM: Reattach yarn, K6 (6, 7), PU 3 sts in CO edge. Rep for **LM**. Turn.

Sl mittens behind both cables. [9 (9, 10) sts per half]

Row 2 (24" needles): LM: With RH needle tip, PU 1 st in CO edge, K7 (7, 8). Rep for **RM**. Turn. [8 (8, 9) sts per half]

[17 (17, 19) sts total per thumb]

Knit even for 5 rnds.

Next rnd:

Row 1: RM: *K1, P1; rep from * to last 1 (1, 0) st, K1f&b (K1f&b, K0). Rep for **LM**. Turn. [10 sts per half]

Row 2: LM: *K1, P1; rep from * to last 0 (0, 1) sts, K0 (K0, K1f&b). Rep for **RM**. Turn. [8 (8, 10) sts per half]

Work in K1, P1 ribbing for 3 more rnds or until desired length. BO in patt.

Weave in ends.

CABLE BELT

The cable belt is worked for one mitten at a time.

Right Mitten

Hold RM with cuff on the right, finger ribbing on the left, and thumb on the bottom. This will be the back of the hand for RM.

With 16" needle and A, PU sts for belt between markers as follows:

Sl needle tip through upper strand of right marked st and knit. Rep for next 9 sts, ending with left marked st. If you cannot pick up 10 sts comfortably, inc to 10 sts in row 1 with a M1L.

Picked-up stitches shown using pink yarn for visibility

Setup row: Purl.

Row 1 (RS): Knit. Turn.

Row 2 (WS) and all even-numbered rows: K1, P8, K1.

Row 3: P1, 4/4 RC, P1.

Rows 5 and 7: P1, K8, P1.

Row 9: P1, 4/4 RC, P1.

Row 10: K1, P8, K1.

Work rows 5–10 twice more; then work rows 5–7 once. Belt should be long enough to reach across back of hand. You may stretch it slightly to fit.

Finishing

Using the three-needle bind off (page 16), attach live sts from belt to mitten as follows. With 24" needle, sl needle tip through lower strand of right marked st. Do not knit. Rep for next 9 sts, ending with left marked st.

Sl cable sts to needle tip and align with 24" needle between markers on mitten at open end of cable belt. Sl RH needle tip through first cable st on LH needle tip and cont through lower strand of right marked mitten st and knit tog; 1 st sits on RH needle. Rep for next cable and mitten sts, then BO 1 st on RH needle. Cont to BO rem sts. Cut yarn and weave in ends.

Cable belt shown in pink

Left Mitten

Hold LM with cuff on the left, finger ribbing on the right, and thumb on the bottom. This will be the back of the hand for LM. PU 10 sts and work cable belt as for RM. Finish as for RM.

KNITTED BLOSSOM (MAKE 2.)

With straight needles and B, using the cable CO (page 11), *CO 11 sts; then immediately BO 10 sts. (1 st)

Hold needle with st in RH, and gently straighten bound-off petal strip. Sl LH needle through outermost strand of yarn from the bottom up at opposite end of strip and knit it. There are 2 sts on RH needle, BO 1 st, sl rem st back to LH needle.

A petal of the knitted blossom worked in pink

Work from * 4 more times. CO 10 sts only each time. On last rep, BO all sts leaving a 10" tail.

Sl tail onto tapestry needle and loosely weave it through blossom center. Pull tail tight and attach to belt; fluff into shape. Weave in ends.

Use beading needle to attach three strands of embroidery thread to center of blossom. Thread three beads on each strand, secure with a double knot, and clip thread close to knot.

firecracker

I've always loved sparkle in things. Honestly, I usually love it a bit too much, and yes, my crafted things border on being kitschy at times. But I'm working on that. These days, glitter is a hot commodity when it comes to accessories, and there is nothing gaudy about the subtle shimmer you'll find in the newest yarns. Despite their metallic content they remain soft and pliable, and their sparkle always adds just the right touch of glamour.

Skill level: Intermediate ■■■◻

Sizes: Women's Small (Medium, Large)

To fit hand circumference up to: 6¾ (7¼, 7¾)"

MATERIALS

2 balls of Grand Opera from Nashua Handknits (86% wool, 9% viscose, 5% metalized polyester; 1.75 oz/50 g; 128 yds/117 m) in color NGO.4087 Red 🌀3

2 size 4 (3.5 mm) circular needles (16" and 24") or size required to obtain gauge

Cable needle

Point protectors

2 regular and 3 lockable stitch markers

Tapestry needle

Small amount of waste yarn

GAUGE

6 sts = 1" in St st

SPECIAL INSTRUCTIONS

2/1 RPC: Sl 1 st to cn and hold in back, K2, P1 from cn.

2/1 LPC: Sl 2 sts to cn and hold in front, P1, K2 from cn.

2/2 RC: Sl 2 sts to cn and hold in back, K2, K2 from cn.

2/2 LC: Sl 2 sts to cn and hold in front, K2, K2 from cn.

CUFF

CO and set up 49 (49, 56) sts per mitten. Follow instructions for "Setting Up the Needles" (page 20).

Small and Medium

Sl 26 sts to 24" needle, leaving 23 sts on 16" needle.

Large

Divide sts evenly on 16" and 24" needles.

Small and Medium

Setup rnd:

Row 1 (16" needle): RM: (K1, P1, K4, P1) 3 times, K1, P1. Rep for **LM**. Turn.

Row 2 (24" needle): LM: (K4, P1, K1, P1) 3 times, K4, P1. Rep for **RM**. Turn.

Rnd 1:

Row 1: RM: (K1, P1, 2/2 RC, P1) 3 times, K1, P1. Rep for **LM**. Turn.

Row 2: LM: (2/2 RC, P1, K1, P1) 3 times, 2/2 RC, P1. Rep for **RM**. Turn.

Rnds 2–4:

Row 1: RM: (K1, P1, K4, P1) 3 times, K1, P1. Rep for **LM**. Turn.

Row 2: LM: (K4, P1, K1, P1) 3 times, K4, P1. Rep for **RM**. Turn.

Work rnds 1–4 another 2 (3) times, then work rnd 1 once.

Large

Setup rnd:

Row 1 (16" needle): RM: (K1, P1, K4, P1) 4 times. Rep for **LM**. Turn.

Row 2 (24" needle): LM: (K4, P1, K1, P1) 4 times. Rep for **RM**. Turn.

Rnd 1:

Row 1: RM: (K1, P1, 2/2 RC, P1) 4 times. Rep for **LM**. Turn.

Row 2: LM: (2/2 RC, P1, K1, P1) 4 times. Rep for **RM**. Turn.

Rnds 2–4:

Row 1: RM: (K1, P1, K4, P1) 4 times. Rep for **LM**. Turn.

Row 2: LM: (K4, P1, K1, P1) 4 times. Rep for **RM**. Turn.

Work rnds 1–4 another 3 times; then work rnd 1 once.

All Sizes

Cuff measures 1¾ (2, 2)" from CO edge.

Setup rnd:

From now on, the 16" needle carries the palm sts and the 24" needle carries the sts for back of hand.

Small and Medium

Row 1: RM: K1, P1, K1f&b, (K1, P1) 3 times, K1f&b, (K1, P1) 3 times, K1f&b, (K1, P1) 3 times, sl last st on lockable stitch marker. Rep for **LM**. Turn. (25 sts per half)

Row 2: LM: Sl st from marker to LH needle, P1, K1f&b, (K1, P1) 3 times, K2tog, (P1, K1) twice, P1, K2tog, (P1, K1) twice, P1, K2tog, P1, K1, P1. Rep for **RM**. Turn. (25 sts per half)

Large

Row 1: RM: K1, P1, K2tog, (P1, K1) twice, P1, K1f&b, (K1, P1) 3 times, K2tog, (P1, K1) twice, P1, K2tog, P1, K1, P1. Rep for **LM**. Turn. (26 sts per half)

Row 2: LM: K1, P1, K2tog, (P1, K1) twice, P1, K1f&b, (K1, P1) 3 times, K2tog, (P1, K1) twice, P1, K2tog, P1, K1, P1. Rep for **LM**. Turn. (26 sts per half)

All Sizes

[50 (50, 52) sts total per mitten]

Work in K1, P1 ribbing for 3 rnds.

BODY

With palm sts facing, sl a lockable marker into the CO edge to mark RM.

Small and Medium

Setup rnd:

Row 1: RM: K1, ssk 1 (0) time, knit to last 3 sts, K2tog 1 (0) time, K1 (3). Rep for **LM**. Turn. [23 (25) sts per half]

Row 2: LM: P1, (K4, P5) twice, K4, P1, sl last st to lockable marker. Rep for **RM**. Turn. (24 sts per half)

Rnd 1:

Row 1: **RM:** Sl st from marker to LH needle, knit to end. Rep for **LM.** Turn. [24 (26) sts per half]

Row 2: **LM:** P1, (K4, P5) twice, K4, P1. Rep for **RM.** Turn.

Large
Rnd 1:

Row 1: **RM:** Knit. Turn. (26 sts per half)

Row 2: **LM:** K1, P1, (K4, P5) twice, K4, P2. Rep for **RM.** Turn. (26 sts per half)

All Sizes

[48 (50, 52) sts total per mitten] See also chart for cabled portion on back of hand only (page 40).

Rnd 2:

Row 1: Knit. Turn.

Row 2: **LM:** K0 (0, 1), P1, (K4, P5) twice, K4, P1 (1, 2). Rep for **RM.** Turn.

Rnd 3:

Row 1: Knit. Turn.

Row 2: **LM:** K0 (0, 1), P1, (2/2 LC, P5) twice, 2/2 RC, P1 (1, 2). Rep for **RM.** Turn.

Rnd 4:

Row 1: Knit. Turn.

Row 2: **LM:** K0 (0, 1), P1, (K4, P5) twice, K4, P1 (1, 2). Rep for **RM.** Turn.

Rnd 5:

Row 1: Knit. Turn.

Row 2: **LM:** K0 (0, 1), P1, K4, P4, 2/1 RPC, 2/1 LPC, P4, K4, P1 (1, 2). Rep for **RM.** Turn.

Rnd 6:

Row 1: Knit. Turn.

Row 2: **LM:** K0 (0, 1), P1, K4, P4, K2, P2, K2, P4, K4, P1 (1, 2). Rep for **RM.** Turn.

Rnd 7:

Row 1: Knit. Turn.

Row 2: **LM:** K0 (0, 1), P1, 2/2 LC, P3, 2/1 RPC, P2, 2/1 LPC, P3, 2/2 RC, P1 (1, 2). Rep for **RM.** Turn.

Mittens measure approx 3¼ (3½, 3½)" from CO edge.

THUMB GUSSET
Rnd 1 (inc rnd; rnd 8 of cable chart):

Row 1: **RM:** LIR, K1, LIL, pm, knit across rem sts. **LM:** Knit to last 3 sts, pm, LIR, K1, LIL. Turn. [26 (28, 28) sts per half]

Row 2: **LM:** K0 (0, 1), P1, K4, P3, K2, P4, K2, P3, K4, P1 (1, 2). Rep for **RM.** Turn.

From now on, sl markers as you come to them.

Rnd 2 (rnd 9 of cable chart):

Row 1: Knit. Turn.

Row 2: **LM:** K0 (0, 1), P1, K4, P2, 2/1 RPC, P4, 2/1 LPC, P2, K4, P1 (1, 2). Rep for **RM.** Turn.

Rnd 3 (rnd 10 of cable chart):

Row 1: Knit. Turn.

Row 2: **LM:** K0 (0, 1), P1, K4, P2, K2, P6, K2, P2, K4, P1 (1, 2). Rep for **RM.** Turn.

Rnd 4 (inc rnd; rnd 11 of cable chart):

Row 1: **RM:** LIR, K3, LIL, knit to end. **LM:** Knit to marker, LIR, K3, LIL. Turn. [28 (30, 30) sts per half]

Row 2: **LM:** K0 (0, 1), P1, 2/2 LC, P2, 2/1 LPC, P4, 2/1 RPC, P2, 2/2 RC, P1 (1, 2). Rep for **RM.** Turn.

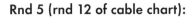

Rnd 5 (rnd 12 of cable chart):

Row 1: Knit. Turn.

Row 2: **LM:** K0 (0, 1), P1, K4, P3, K2, P4, K2, P3, K4, P1 (1, 2). Rep for **RM**. Turn.

Rnd 6 (rnd 13 of cable chart):

Row 1: Knit. Turn.

Row 2: **LM:** K0 (0, 1), P1, K4, P3, 2/1 LPC, P2, 2/1 RPC, P3, K4, P1 (1, 2). Rep for **RM**. Turn.

Rnd 7 (inc rnd; rnd 14 of cable chart):

Row 1: **RM:** LIR, K5, LIL, knit to end. **LM:** Knit to marker, LIR, K5, LIL. Turn. [30 (32, 32) sts per half]

Row 2: **LM:** K0 (0, 1), P1, K4, P4, K2, P2, K2, P4, K4, P1 (1, 2). Rep for **RM**. Turn.

Rnd 8 (rnd 15 of cable chart):

Row 1: Knit. Turn.

Row 2: **LM:** K0 (0, 1), P1, 2/2 LC, P4, 2/1 LPC, 2/1 RPC, P4, 2/2 RC, P1 (1, 2). Rep for **RM**. Turn.

Rnd 9 (rnd 16 of cable chart):

Row 1: Knit. Turn.

Row 2: **LM:** K0 (0, 1), P1, (K4, P5) twice, K4. P1 (1, 2). Rep for **RM**. Turn.

Rnd 10 (inc rnd; rnd 17 of cable chart):

Row 1: **RM:** LIR, K7, LIL, knit to end. **LM:** Knit to marker, LIR, K7, LIL. Turn. [32 (34, 34) sts per half]

Row 2: **LM:** K0 (0, 1), P1, K4, P5, 2/2 LC, P5, K4, P1 (1, 2). Rep for **RM**. Turn.

Rnd 11 (rnd 18 of cable chart):

Row 1: Knit. Turn.

Row 2: **LM:** K0 (0, 1), P1, (K4, P5) twice, K4, P1 (1, 2). Rep for **RM**. Turn.

Rnd 12 (rnd 19 of cable chart):

Row 1: Knit. Turn.

Row 2: **LM:** K0 (0, 1), P1, 2/2 LC, P4, 2/1 RPC, 2/1 LPC, P4, 2/2 RC, P1 (1, 2). Rep for **RM**. Turn.

Rnd 13 (inc rnd; rnd 20 of cable chart):

Row 1: **RM:** LIR, K9, LIL, knit to end. **LM:** Knit to marker, LIR, K9, LIL. Turn. [34 (36, 36) sts per half]

Row 2: **LM:** K0 (0, 1), P1, K4, P4, K2, P2, K2, P4, K4, P1 (1, 2). Rep for **RM**. Turn.

Rnd 14 (rnd 21 of cable chart):

Row 1: Knit. Turn.

Row 2: **LM:** K0 (0, 1), P1, K4, P3, 2/1 RPC, P2, 2/1 LPC, P3, K4, P1 (1, 2). Rep for **RM**. Turn.

Rnd 15 (rnd 22 of cable chart):

Remove markers as you come to them.

Row 1: **RM:** Sl next 13 sts to waste yarn; with backward loop cast on (page 11) CO 3 (3, 4) sts to RH needle. Knit across rem sts. **LM:** Knit to marker, sl next 13 sts to waste yarn; with backward loop cast on (page 11) CO 3 (3, 4) sts to RH needle. Turn. [24 (26, 27) sts per half]

Row 2: **LM:** K0 (0, 1), P1, K4, P3, K2, P4, K2, P3, K4, P1 (1, 2). Rep for **RM**. Turn.

Rnd 16 (rnd 23 of cable chart):

Row 1: Knit. Turn.

Row 2: **LM:** K0 (0, 1), P1, 2/2 LC, P2, 2/1 LPC, P4, 2/1 RPC, P2, 2/2 RC, P1 (1, 2). Rep for **RM**. Turn.

Rnd 17 (rnd 24 of cable chart):

Row 1: Knit. Turn.

Row 2: **LM:** K0 (0, 1), P1, K4, P2, K2, P6, K2, P2, K4, P1 (1, 2). Rep for **RM**. Turn.

Rnd 18 (rnd 25 of cable chart):

Row 1: Knit. Turn.

Row 2: **LM:** K0 (0, 1), P1, K4, P2, 2/1 LPC, P4, 2/1 RPC, P2, K4, P1 (1, 2). Rep for **RM**. Turn.

Rnd 19 (rnd 26 of cable chart):

Row 1: Knit. Turn.

Row 2: **LM:** K0 (0, 1), P1, K4, P3, K2, P4, K2, P3, K4, P1 (1, 2). Rep for **RM**. Turn.

Rnd 20 (rnd 27 of cable chart):

Row 1: Knit. Turn.

Row 2: **LM:** K0 (0, 1), P1, 2/2 LC, P3, 2/1 LPC, P2, 2/1 RPC, P3, 2/2 RC, P1 (1, 2). Rep for **RM**. Turn.

Rnd 21 (rnd 28 of cable chart):

Row 1: Knit. Turn.

Row 2: **LM:** K0 (0, 1), P1, K4, P4, K2, P2, K2, P4, K4, P1 (1, 2). Rep for **RM**. Turn.

Rnd 22 (rnd 29 of cable chart):

Row 1: Knit. Turn.

Row 2: **LM:** K0 (0, 1), P1, K4, P4, 2/1 LPC, 2/1 RPC, P4, K4, P1 (1, 2). Rep for **RM**. Turn.

Rnd 23 (rnd 30 of cable chart):

Row 1: Knit. Turn.

Row 2: **LM:** K0 (0, 1), P1, (K4, P5) twice, K4. P1 (1, 2). Rep for **RM**. Turn.

Rnd 24 (rnd 31 of cable chart):

Row 1: Knit. Turn.

Row 2: **LM:** K0 (0, 1), P1, 2/2 LC, P5, 2/2 LC, P5, 2/2 RC, P1 (1, 2). Rep for **RM**. Turn.

Rnd 25 (rnd 32 of cable chart):

Row 1: Knit. Turn.

Row 2: **LM:** K0 (0, 1), P1, (K4, P5) twice, K4, P1 (1, 2). Rep for **RM**. Turn.

Rnd 26:

Row 1: **RM:** K1 (1, 0),(K2tog) 0 (0, 1) times, P1, *K1, P1; rep from * to end. Rep for **LM**. Turn. [24 (26, 26) sts per half]

Row 2: *K1, P1; rep from * to end. Turn.

Work in K1, P1 ribbing for 1" or desired length.

Next rnd:

Row 1: **RM:** Cut yarn, leaving a 21" tail. BO in patt until 1 st is left on RH needle, sl st onto lockable marker. Rep for **LM**. Turn.

Row 2: **LM:** Sl st from marker to RH needle, cont BO of rem sts on 24" needle in patt. Rep for **RM**.

Weave in ends.

THUMB

Setup

RM: With palm facing, sl 6 sts from waste yarn to 16" needle, beg at thumb gusset and working toward mitten body. **LM:** Cont with same needle tip, sl 6 sts from waste yarn to 16" needle, beg at mitten body and working toward thumb gusset. Turn.

LM: With back of hands facing, sl rem 7 sts from waste yarn to 24" needle. Rep for **RM**. Turn.

(13 sts total per thumb)

Connect the two mittens with a piece of scrap yarn or a lockable marker right above the cuff to keep them close together as you work. Make sure to slip mittens behind needle cables and out of the way each time you turn your work.

Rnd 1:

Row 1 (16" needle): RM: Reattach yarn, K6, PU 2 sts across CO edge. **LM:** Reattach yarn, cont with same needle tip PU 2 sts across CO edge, K6. Turn. (8 sts per half)

Row 2 (24" needle): LM: K7, PU 1 (1, 3) st across CO edge. **RM:** PU 1 (1, 3) st across CO edge, K7. Turn. [8 (8, 10) sts per half]

[16 (16, 18) sts total per thumb]

Rnds 2–5: Knit.

Rnds 6–10: *K1, P1; rep from * to end.

Next rnd:

Row 1: RM: Cut yarn, leaving a 10" tail. BO in patt until 1 st is left on RH needle, sl st onto lockable marker. Rep for **LM.** Turn.

Row 2: LM: Sl marker to RH needle, BO rem sts on 24" needle in patt. Rep for **RM.**

Weave in ends.

Cable Chart

Small and Medium: Work between dark lines on back of hand.
Large: Work all sts on back of hand.

Key

☐	K
•	P
⟋	2/2 RC
⟍	2/2 LC
⟋•	2/1 RPC
⟍•	2/1 LPC

Chart rows numbered 1–32 (right side), columns numbered 26 25 24 23 22 21 20 19 18 17 16 15 14 13 12 11 10 9 8 7 6 5 4 3 2 1.

I'm a very touchy-feely person. When I go shopping I pretty much have to touch everything! I don't carry a purse. I prefer a backpack or shoulder pouch to hold my stuff because it's hands-free! So why wouldn't I want free and easy use of my thumbs, the wonderful little appendages that help me grab and hold things? If you feel the same way I do, get ready to dabble with hoodies and free your thumbs from their confinement forever.

Skill level: Intermediate ◼◼◼▢

Sizes: Women's Small (Medium, Large)

To fit hand circumference up to: 6¾ (7¼, 7¾)"

MATERIALS

2 skeins of Merino Worsted from Abuelita (100% merino wool; 3.5 oz/100 g; 218 yds/200 m) in color 1029 Candy ⓿

2 size 8 (5 mm) circular needles (16" and 24") or size required to obtain gauge

2 size 8 (5 mm) double-pointed needles

Cable needle

2 buttons, approx 1" diameter

Point protectors

2 regular and 2 lockable stitch markers

Tapestry needle

Small amount of waste yarn

GAUGE

3.75 sts = 1" in St st

SPECIAL INSTRUCTIONS

2/1 LC: Slip 1 st to cn and hold in front, K2, K1 from cn.

CUFF

CO and set up 30 (30, 35) sts [15 (15, 15) sts on 16" needle; 15 (15, 20) sts on 24" needle]. Follow instructions for "Setting Up the Needles" (page 20).

Setup rnd:

Row 1 (16" needle): RM: K3, pm, P2, (K3, P2) twice. Rep for **LM**. Turn.

Row 2 (24" needle): LM: K3, P2, (K3, P2) 2 (2, 3) times. Rep for **RM**. Turn.

Rnd 1: *(2/1 LC, P2); rep from * to end.

Rnds 2–4: *(K3, P2); rep from * to end.

Rep rnds 1–4 until cuff measures 2" or desired length, ending with rnd 4. Rep rnd 2 once more.

BODY

Medium

Inc rnd: *K1, M1R, K14; rep from * to end. (32 sts total per mitten)

All Sizes

Knit even until mittens measure 3 (3¼, 3½)" from CO edge.

THUMB GUSSET

Rnd 1:

Row 1: RM: K1f&b, K1, K1f&b, knit to end. **LM:** Knit to last 3 sts, pm, K1f&b, K1, K1f&b. Turn. [17 (18, 17) sts per half]

Row 2: Knit.

Rnd 2: Knit.

Rnd 3:

Row 1: RM: K1f&b, K3, K1f&b, knit to end. **LM:** Knit to marker, K1f&b, K3, K1f&b. Turn. [19 (20, 19) sts per half]

Row 2: Knit.

Rnd 4: Knit.

Rnd 5:

Row 1: RM: K1f&b, K5, K1f&b, knit to end. **LM:** Knit to marker, K1f&b, K5, K1f&b. Turn. [21 (22, 21) sts per half]

Row 2: Knit.

Rnd 6: Knit.

Rnd 7:

Row 1: RM: K1f&b, K7, K1f&b, knit to end. **LM:** Knit to marker, K1f&b, K7, K1f&b. Turn. [23 (24, 23) sts per half]

Row 2: Knit.

Rnd 8: Knit.

Rnd 9:

Row 1: RM: K1, sl next 10 sts to waste yarn, with backward loop cast on (page 11), CO 2 sts to RH needle. Knit to end. **LM:** Knit to marker and remove. K1, sl next 10 sts to waste yarn. Cont with same needle tip, CO 2 sts using backward loop cast on. Turn. [15 (16, 15) sts per half]

Row 2: Knit. Turn. [15 (16, 20) sts per half]

Knit even until mittens measure approx 4½ (5, 5½)" from CO edge or 2" less than desired length.

MITTEN HOODIE SETUP

Rnd 1:

Row 1: Knit. Turn.

*Knit into shoulder of st below as if to LIR but do not knit corresponding st on LH needle. Instead sl it pw to RH needle; rep from * to end. Rep for **RM**. Turn. [30 (32, 40) sts per half]

Rnd 2:

Row 1: Knit. Turn.

Row 2: LM: Hold 2 dpns parallel to each other in right hand. Work across 24" needle, alternately slipping inc sts to back dpn and sl sts to front dpn. Rep for **RM**. [15 (16, 20) sts per dpn]

LM: Sl sts pw from front dpn to waste yarn. With 24" needle, knit across sts on back dpn. Rep for **RM**. Turn.

BODY

Knit even until mitten measures approx 5 (5½, 6)" from CO edge or 1" less than desired length.

Medium

Dec rnd:

Row 1: RM: K1, K2tog, K13. Rep for **LM.** Turn. (15 sts per half)

Row 2: LM: K13, K2tog, K1. Rep for **RM.** Turn. (15 sts per half)

All Sizes

Next rnd: *K3, P2; rep from * to end.

Work in K3, P2 ribbing until work measures approx 6½ (7, 7½)" from CO edge or desired length. BO as for "Basic Fingerless Mittens" (page 27).

THUMB

Setup

RM: With thumb gusset on right and hoodie sts in back of mitten, sl 4 sts from waste yarn, beg at thumb gusset and working toward mitten body. **LM:** With thumb gusset on left and hoodie sts in back, cont with same needle tip, sl 6 sts to needle beg at mitten body. Turn.

LM: With thumb gusset on right and hoodie sts facing, sl rem 4 sts from waste yarn to 24" needle. **RM:** With thumb to left and hoodie sts facing, cont with same needle tip, sl rem 6 sts from waste yarn to needle. Turn. (10 sts total per thumb)

Connect the two mittens with a piece of scrap yarn or a lockable marker right above the cuff to keep them close together as you work. Make sure to slip mittens behind needle cables and out of the way each time you turn your work.

Rnd 1:

Row 1 (16" needle): RM: Reattach yarn, K4, PU 2 sts in CO edge. **LM:** With RH needle, PU 2 sts in CO edge, then K6. Turn.

Row 2 (24" needle): LM: K4, PU 2 sts in CO edge. **RM:** With RH needle tip, PU 2 sts in CO edge, K6. Turn.

(14 sts total per thumb)

Knit even for 2 rnds.

Next rnd:

Sts for LM must be shifted to accommodate thumb hoodie setup.

Row 1: RM: K6. **LM:** K2 and put sts on lockable marker, K6. Turn. (6 sts per half)

Row 2: LM: K6, sl sts from marker to LH needle, K2. **RM:** K8. Turn. (8 sts per half)

THUMB HOODIE SETUP

Rnd 1:

Row 1: Knit. Turn.

*Knit into shoulder of st below as if to LIR but do not knit corresponding st on LH needle. Instead sl it pw to RH needle; rep from * to end. Turn. Rep for **RM.** Turn. (16 sts total per half)

Rnd 2:

Row 1: Knit. Turn.

Row 2: LM: Hold 2 dpns parallel to each other in right hand. Work across 24" needle, alternately slipping inc sts to back dpn and sl sts to front dpn. (8 sts per dpn)

LM: Sl sts pw from front dpn to waste yarn. With 24" needle, knit across sts on back dpn. Rep for **RM.** Turn.

FINISH THUMB

Work in K1, P1 ribbing for 3 rnds or desired length. BO.

MITTEN HOODIE

Setup

RM: With back of hands (RS) facing, sl 15 (16, 20) sts from waste yarn to 16" needle. Reattach yarn and knit across. Cont with same needle tip and using the backward loop cast on (page 11), CO 15 (16, 15) sts. Sl these 15 (16, 15) sts pw to 24" needle. Fold needles so both tips face in same direction and open end of CO edge as well as working yarn face toward cables. Follow instructions for "Setting Up the Needles" (page 20).

Sl mitten body behind needle cables; sts on 16" needle are attached to mitten and sts on 24" needle are not.

LM: With back of hands facing and **RM** to right of needle tip, sl 15 (16, 20) sts pw from waste yarn to 16" needle. Both mittens are on 16" needle. Do not turn. Beg with **RM** and sl all sts from LH to RH needle. Reattach yarn for **LM** and knit across. Cont with same needle tip and using backward loop cast on, CO 15 (16, 15) sts. Sl these 15 (16, 15) sts to 24" needle. Fold needles so both tips face to left and open end of CO edge as well as working yarn face toward cables. Follow instructions for "Setting Up the Needles (page 20).

[30 (32, 35) sts total per hoodie; 15 (16, 20) sts on 16" needle; 15 (16, 15) sts on 24" needle]

Small and Large

Rnd 1: *K3, P2; rep from * to end.

Medium

Rnd 1:

Row 1: RM: K1, K2tog, K1, P2, (K3, P2) twice. Rep for **LM.** Turn. (15 sts per half)

Row 2: LM: (K3, P2) twice, K1, K2tog, K1, P2. Rep for **RM.** Turn. (15 sts per half)

All Sizes

Rnd 2: *K3, P2; rep from * to end.

Rnd 3: *2/1 LC, P2; rep from * to end.

Rnds 4–6: Rep rnd 2.

Rnd 7: *2/1 LC, P2; rep from * to end.

Medium

Inc rnd:

Row 1: RM: K1, M1R, K14. Rep for **LM.** Turn. (16 sts per half)

Row 2: LM: K1, M1R, K14. Rep for **RM.** Turn. (16 sts per half)

All Sizes

Knit even until hoodie measures 2½" from CO edge or 1½" less than desired length.

HOODIE CROWN

Small and Large

Rnd 1: *K3, K2tog; rep from * to end. [24 (28) sts total per hoodie]

Rnds 2 and 3: Knit.

Rnd 4: *K2, K2tog; rep from * to end. [18 (21) sts total per hoodie]

Rnds 5 and 6: Knit.

Rnd 7: *K1, K2tog; rep from * to end. [12 (14) sts total per hoodie]

Rnds 8 and 9: Knit.

Small

Rnd 10: *K1, K2tog; rep from * to end. (8 sts total per hoodie)

Large

Rnd 10:

Row 1: RM: *K1, K2tog; rep from * to end. Rep for **LM**. Turn. (4 sts per half)

Row 2: LM: (K2tog) 4 times. Rep for **RM**. Turn. (4 sts per half)

Small and Large

Rnd 11: Knit.

Rnd 12: *K2tog; rep from * to end. (4 sts total per hoodie)

Rnd 13:

Row 1: RM: K2tog, sl st to lockable marker. Rep for **LM**. Turn.

Row 2: LM: Sl st from marker to LH needle, K2tog, K1. Rep for **RM**. Turn. (2 sts total per hoodie)

Medium

Rnd 1: *K6, K2tog; rep from * to end. (28 sts total per hoodie)

Rnds 2 and 3: Knit.

Rnd 4: *K5, K2tog; rep from * to end. (24 sts total per hoodie)

Rnds 5 and 6: Knit.

Rnd 7: *K4, K2tog; rep from * to end. (20 sts total per hoodie)

Rnd 8: Knit.

Rnd 9: *K3, K2tog; rep from * to end. (16 sts total per hoodie)

Rnd 10: Knit.

Rnd 11: *K2, K2tog; rep from * to end. (12 sts total per hoodie)

Rnd 12: *K1, K2tog; rep from * to end. (8 sts total per hoodie)

Rnd 13: *K2tog; rep from * to end. (4 sts total per hoodie)

Rnd 14:

Row 1: RM: K2tog, move st to lockable marker. Rep for **LM**. Turn.

Row 2: LM: Sl st from marker to LH needle, K2tog, K1. Rep for **RM**. (2 sts total per hoodie)

All Sizes

RM: Sl sts from 24" needle to dpn, make sure working yarn sits at needle tip. Beg I-cord (page 14) and work for 2¾ to 3". Cut 8" tail and pull through to WS, forming a button loop with I-cord, secure. Rep for **LM**.

THUMB HOODIE

Setup

RM: With back of hands facing, sl 8 sts from waste yarn to 16" needle. Reattach yarn and knit across. Cont with same needle tip and using the backward loop cast on, CO 6 sts. Sl these 6 sts pw to 24" needle. Fold needles so both tips face in same direction and open end of CO edge as well as working yarn face toward cables. Follow instructions for "Setting Up the Needles" (page 20).

Sl thumb behind needle cables; sts on 16" needle are attached to mitten and sts on 24" needle are not.

LM: With back of hands facing and **RM** to right of needle tip, sl 8 sts pw from waste yarn to 16" needle.

Both mittens sit on 16" needle. Beg with **RM** and sl all sts from LH to RH needle. Reattach yarn for **LM**, and knit across. Cont with same needle tip and using backward loop cast on, CO 6 sts. Sl these 6 sts to 24" needle. Fold needles so both tips face to left and open end of CO edge as well as working yarn face toward cables. Follow instructions for "Setting Up the Needles" (page 20).

(14 sts total per hoodie; 8 sts on 16" needle; 6 sts on 24" needle)

Work in K1, P1 ribbing for 3 rnds. Knit even for 4 (5, 5) rnds.

THUMB HOODIE CROWN

All Sizes

Rnd 1:

Row 1: **RM:** (K2, K2tog) twice. Rep for **LM**. Turn. (6 sts per half)

Row 2: **LM:** (K1, K2tog) twice. Rep for **RM**. Turn. (4 sts per half)

Rnd 2: *K2tog; rep from * to end. (5 sts total per hoodie)

Rnd 3:

Row 1: **RM:** (K2tog) and sl rem st on lockable marker. Rep for **LM**. Turn.

Row 2: **LM:** Sl st from marker to RH needle. Cut yarn and thread tail on tapestry needle, then sl through rem sts. Cinch tight and bring to WS. Rep for **RM**. Weave in ends. Sew buttons opposite loops.

double-stuff mittens

Most mittens look great on the outside, but despite Tennessee's relatively mild winters, they never really keep my hands warm. Even when they're worked with bulky yarn, the toasty feeling I desire eludes my fingers. This pair, however, is *heavenly* and unbelievably cozy inside, and will leave you saying, "Wow!" Using Cascade Yarns' lovely Eco Alpaca for the lining and their slightly heavier Eco Duo Alpaca for the outer shell, you can stitch these mittens with amazing results—a deliciously soft and snug sanctuary to keep your hands warm and protected.

Skill level: Intermediate ■■■□

Sizes: Women's Small (Medium, Large)

To fit hand circumference up to: 6¾ (7¼, 7¾)"

MATERIALS

A 1 skein of Eco Alpaca from Cascade Yarns (100% undyed baby alpaca; 3.5 oz/100 g; 220 yds/200 m) in color 1510 (4)

B 1 skein of Eco Duo from Cascade Yarns (70% baby alpaca, 30% merino wool-undyed; 3.5 oz/100 g; 197 yds/180 m) in color 1706 (4)

2 size 2 (2.75 mm) and 2 size 6 (4 mm) circular needles (16" and 24") or size required to obtain gauge

1 size 4 (3.5 mm) straight needle

Size F-5 (3.75 mm) crochet hook

Point protectors

3 lockable stitch markers

Tapestry needle

Small amount of waste yarn

GAUGE

6 sts = 1" in St st using smaller needles and A

5½ sts = 1" in St st using larger needles and B

MITTEN LINING
Cuff

Setup rnd:

Row 1: RM: Using 1 straight needle, crochet hook, waste yarn, and provisional cast on (page 11), CO 40 (40, 44) sts. Switch to smaller 16" circular needle and A, knit all 40 (40, 44) sts, then sl 20 (20, 24) sts to 24" needle, starting with last worked st on 16" needle. Cont setup for **RM** as for first mitten in "Basic Fingerless Mittens" (page 20).

Row 2: LM: CO as for **RM**; then cont setup as for second mitten in "Basic Fingerless Mittens" pattern.

Work in K2, P2 ribbing until cuffs measure 2½ (3, 3)".

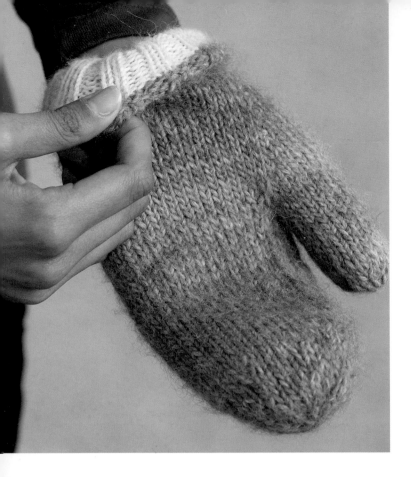

Medium

Row 1 (16" needle): RM: K7, M1R, K6, M1R, K7. Rep for **LM**. Turn. (22 sts per half)

Row 2 (24" needle): LM: K7, M1R, K6, M1R, K7. Rep for **RM**. Turn. (22 sts per half)

Next rnd: Knit.

Large

Row 1 (16" needle): RM: K7, M1R, K6, M1R, K7. Rep for **LM**. Turn. (22 sts per half)

Row 2 (24" needle): LM: K1 and sl to lockable marker, knit to end. Rep for **RM**. Turn. (23 sts per half)

Next rnd:

Row 1: RM: Knit, sl st from marker to LH needle, K1. Rep for **LM**. Turn. (23 sts per half)

Row 2: Knit. (23 sts per half)

All Sizes

[42 (44, 46) sts total per mitten]

Knit 1 rnd.

Body

Knit 1 rnd.

Inc rnd:

Small

Row 1 (16" needle): RM: K1, M1R, knit to end. Rep for **LM**. Turn. (21 sts per half)

Row 2 (24" needle): LM: K1, M1R, knit to end. Rep for **RM**. Turn. (21 sts per half)

Next rnd: Knit.

Thumb Gusset

Rnd 1:

Row 1: RM: K1, M1R, K1, M1L, knit to end. Rep for **LM**. Turn. [23 (24, 25) sts per half]

Row 2: Knit. Turn.

Rnds 2 and 3: Knit.

Rnd 4:

Row 1: RM: K1, M1R, K3, M1L, knit to end. Rep for **LM**. Turn. [25 (26, 27) sts per half]

Row 2: Knit. Turn.

Rnds 5 and 6: Knit.

Rnd 7:

Row 1: **RM:** K1, M1R, K5, M1L, knit to end. Rep for **LM**. Turn. [27 (28, 29) sts per half]

Row 2: Knit. Turn.

Rnds 8 and 9: Knit.

Rnd 10:

Row 1: **RM:** K1, M1R, K7, M1L, knit to end. Rep for **LM**. Turn. [29 (30, 31) sts per half]

Row 2: Knit. Turn.

Rnds 11 and 12: Knit.

Rnd 13:

Row 1: **RM:** K1, M1R, K9, M1L, knit to end. Rep for **LM**. Turn. [31 (32, 33) sts per half]

Row 2: Knit. Turn.

Rnds 14 and 15: Knit.

Rnd 16:

Row 1: **RM:** K1, M1R, K11, M1L, knit to end. Rep for **LM**. Turn. [33 (34, 35) sts per half]

Row 2: Knit. Turn.

Rnds 17 and 18: Knit.

Large

Rnd 19:

Row 1: **RM:** K1, M1R, K13, M1L, knit to end. Rep for **LM**. Turn. (37 sts per half)

Row 2: Knit. Turn.

Rnds 20 and 21: Knit.

All Sizes

Next rnd:

Row 1: **RM:** Sl 15 (15, 17) sts to waste yarn and using backward loop cast on (page 11), CO 3 sts to RH needle tip. Knit to end. Rep for **LM**. Turn. [21 (22, 23) sts per half]

Row 2: Knit. Turn. [21 (22, 23) sts per half]

Mittens measure approx 5¾ (5¾, 6)" from CO edge.

Knit even until mittens measure approx 9 (9¼, 9½)" from CO edge.

Dec rnd:

Small

Row 1: **RM:** K1, ssk, knit to end. Rep for **LM**. Turn. (20 sts per half)

Row 2: **LM:** K1, ssk, knit to end. Rep for **RM**. Turn. (20 sts per half)

Medium

Row 1: **RM:** K1, ssk, knit to last 3 sts, K2tog, K1. Rep for **LM**. Turn. (20 sts per half)

Row 2: **LM:** K1, ssk, knit to last 3 sts, K2tog, K1. Rep for **RM**. Turn. (20 sts per half)

Large

Row 1: **RM:** K1, ssk, (K7, K2tog) twice, K2. Rep for **LM**. Turn. (20 sts per half)

Row 2: **LM:** K1, ssk, (K7, K2tog) twice, K2. Rep for **RM**. Turn. (20 sts per half)

Crown

All Sizes

(40 sts total per mitten)

Rnd 1: Knit.

Rnd 2: *K3, K2tog; rep from * to end. (32 sts total per mitten)

Rnds 3–5: Knit.

Rnd 6: *K2, K2tog; rep from * to end. (24 sts total per mitten)

Rnds 7–9: Knit.

Rnd 10: *K1, K2tog; rep from * to end. (16 sts total per mitten)

Rnd 11: Knit.

Rnd 12: *K2tog; rep from * to end. (8 sts total per mitten)

Cut yarn, leaving a 10" tail. Using tapestry needle, sl tail through rem sts of **RM,** change tapestry needle to tail for **LM** and rep. Turn and sl needle through rem sts for **LM.** Cinch tight and bring to inside of mitten. Rep for **RM.** Weave in ends.

Mittens measure approx 10 (10¼, 10½)" from CO edge.

Thumb

Setup

RM: With thumb gusset on right side and marker facing, sl 7 (7, 8) sts from waste yarn to 16" needle, beg at thumb gusset and working toward mitten body. **LM:** With thumb gusset on right side, cont with same needle tip, sl 7 (7, 8) sts from waste yarn to 16" needle, beg at thumb gusset and working toward mitten body. Turn.

LM: With thumb gusset on left side, sl rem 8 (8, 9) sts from waste yarn to 24" needle. Cont with same needle tip and rep for **RM.** Turn.

[15 (15, 17) sts total per thumb]

Connect the two mittens with a piece of scrap yarn or a lockable st marker right above the cuff to keep them close together as you work. Make sure to slip mittens behind needle cables and out of the way each time you turn your work.

Rnd 1:

Row 1 (16" needle): **RM:** Reattach yarn, K7 (7, 8), PU 3 sts across CO edge. Rep for **LM.** Turn. [10 (10, 11) sts per half]

Row 2 (24" needle): **LM:** With RH needle tip, PU 1 st across CO edge, K8 (8, 9). Rep for **RM.** Turn. [9 (9, 10) sts per half]

[19 (19, 21) sts total per thumb]

Sl a lockable st marker through 1 st of last worked rnd on each thumb to help measure length. Knit even until thumb measures approx 1½ (1¾, 2)" from marker.

Thumb Crown

Small and Medium

Rnd 1:

Row 1: **RM:** (K1, K2tog) 3 times, K1. Rep for **LM.** Turn. (7 sts per half)

Row 2: **LM:** K1, K2tog, K3, K2tog, K1. Rep for **RM.** Turn. (7 sts per half)

Large

Rnd 1:

Row 1: **RM:** (K2tog, K1) 3 times, K2tog. Rep for **LM**. Turn. (7 sts per half)

Row 2: **LM:** (K1, K2tog) 3 times, K1. Rep for **RM**. Turn. (7 sts per half)

All Sizes

Rnds 2 and 3: Knit.

Rnd 4: *(K1, K2tog) twice, K1; rep from * to end. (10 sts total per thumb)

Cut yarn, leaving a 10" tail. Using tapestry needle, sl tail through rem sts of **RM,** change tapestry needle to tail for **LM** and rep. Turn and sl needle through rem sts for **LM**. Cinch tight and bring to inside of mitten. Rep for **RM**. Weave in ends.

OUTER SHELL

Turn first mitten upside down with thumb and crochet tail on right. Looking at the inside of mitten, notice the purl sts of lining sitting within provisional CO on WS of cuff.

Provisional cast on shown in yellow; lining shown in pink for clarity

Clip crochet tail (to right) next to first purl st (to left), and *carefully scoop up st from back to front using larger 24" circular needle. Pick out any small pieces of clipped tail slowly. One will be attached to next st on LH needle; don't pull it yet. Instead insert needle through st from back to front (2 sts sit on RH needle) and pull provisional yarn from these sts, leaving just the live sts on the needle. Cont with same needle tip and rep for **LM**. Rep from * until 20 (20, 24) live sts sit on RH needle. Turn work. With thumb on left, cont to move rem 20 (20, 20) sts of **LM** to larger 16" needle.

Provisional cast on (yellow) being pulled from live lining sts (pink)

Slide mitten to right of needle tips and onto cable. Cont with same needle tip and rep for **RM**. Turn. 16" needle ready to be worked, thumbs on right.

With B, knit 2 rnds, then purl 1 rnd. Work as for lining, beg with ribbing on cuff. Push lining into completed outer shell and tug into place. Take care to catch both layers when fastening off crowns of mittens and thumb, securing lining to outer shell.

little thrummer set

The iciest winter is no match for thrummed anything! Wearing cozy thrummed accessories is like sticking your hands into a warm pile of roving or covering your head with a soft fleece. I was addicted to that feeling from the moment I started working with little thrums and knitted obsessively until the set was finished. Embarrassingly enough, I had to (yes, *had to*) try them on after each row, closing my eyes and smiling as I marveled again and again at how good they felt around my hands.

Skill level: Easy ◖■☐◗

Hat sizes: Women's Extra Small/Small (Medium/Large)

To fit head circumference up to: 20–21 (22–23)"

Mitten sizes: Women's Small (Medium, Large)

To fit hand circumference up to: 6¾ (7¼, 7¾)"

MATERIALS

Shepherd Worsted from Lorna's Laces (100% superwash merino wool; 3.5 oz/100 g; 225 yds/206 m) 〔4〕

A 1 skein in color 11ns Bold Red

B 1 skein in color 10ns Peach

.75 oz/20 g of pink roving; 1.5 oz/40 g of red roving

For Extra Small or Small hat: 2 size 5 (3.75 mm) circular needles (16" and 24")

For Medium or Large hat; all mittens: 2 size 6 (4 mm) circular needles (16" and 24") or size required to obtain gauge

4½" by 6" piece of cardboard (for tassel)

Point protectors

2 regular and 5 lockable stitch markers

Tapestry needle

Small amount of waste yarn

GAUGE

5 sts = 1" in St st using larger needles

SPECIAL INSTRUCTIONS

K1B (Knit 1 below): K1 in center of st below the next st on the LH needle. After knitting in the st below, slip the st off the LH needle.

RT (Right twist): K2tog but don't slide sts off LH needle. Instead knit st closest to needle tip again; now slide both sts off LH needle.

T1 (Thrum 1): Insert thrum in next st as directed on page 56. Use contrasting color roving in each st.

Thrum

1. Pull (don't cut!) a 5" to 6" tuft from roving.

2. Form a ring, bringing ends together so they overlap slightly.

3. First twist overlapping ends together between fingers; then twist the middle of thrum. It should be about as thick as the mitten yarn.

4. Insert needle into st to be thrummed; then lay thrum over needle at the center twist, and hold both ends parallel to LH needle in left hand. Guide working yarn behind thrum and knit st normally.

5. Thrum and st sit next to each other on RH needle. ALWAYS knit them tog tbl in next rnd. Tug thrums snugly into place if necessary.

Tassel

Cut 2 strands of A 12" long and set aside. Cut a 4½" x 6" piece of cardboard, and holding 1 strand of A and 1 strand of B together wrap yarn around shorter side 40 times. Slip a 12" piece under the wrapped strands at one end of cardboard and tie it tight and secure around the 40 strands. Do not cut tails.

Slip yarn from cardboard (it will look like a mini skein), and wrap the other 12" strand around it several times about 1" below the first tie. Fasten yarn securely into place. Cut through all loops at bottom of tassel; trim strands if necessary. Sew tassel to center of hat crown using the tails of each tie. Weave in ends and gently fluff tassel with fingers.

HAT

The band pattern used in my thrummed hat and mittens has a 13-stitch repeat, which doesn't leave any room to adjust the stitch count for subtle size changes. I therefore used different-sized needles instead. Using the smaller needle will allow you to tighten the fabric and create a smaller hat; using the larger needle will loosen the fabric, creating a larger hat.

Brim

With smaller (larger) 16" circular needle and A, CO 104 sts, pm, and being careful not to twist, close rnd.

Knit 6 rnds, then cut A.

Change to B and purl 1 rnd.

Band

Rnd 1: *(RT) 3 times, (P1, K1) 3 times, P1; rep from * to end.

Rnd 2: *K6, (P1, K1) 3 times, P1; rep from * to end.

Rnd 3: *K1, (RT) twice, (K1, P1) 4 times; rep from * to end.

Rnd 4: Rep rnd 2.

Rep rnds 1–4 once more. Cut B.

Thrummed Body

With A, purl 1 rnd, then knit 1 rnd.

Inc rnd: K5, M1, K10, M1, (K11, M1, K10, M1) 4 times, K5. (114 sts total for hat)

Rnd 1: *K5, T1; rep from * to end.

Remember to always knit thrum and regular st tog tbl.

Rnds 2–6: Knit.

Rep rnds 1–6 once more, then work rnds 1–3 once more. Cut A.

Rnds 16–18: With B, knit.

Rnd 19: *K5, T1; rep from * to end.

Rnds 20–24: Knit.

Rnd 25: *K5, T1; rep from * to end.

Rnds 26–28: Knit. Cut B.

Rnds 29 and 30: With A, knit.

Rnd 31: *K5, T1; rep from * to end.

Rnds 32 and 33: Knit. Cut A.

Rnds 34–36: With B, knit.

Rnd 37: *K5, T1; rep from * to end.

Rnd 38: Knit.

Crown

Rnd 1: K13, K2tog, K27, K2tog, K26, K2tog, K27, K2tog, K13. (110 sts total for hat)

Rnd 2: Knit.

Rnd 3: *K8, K2tog; rep from * to end. (99 sts total for hat)

Rnd 4: Knit.

Rnd 5: K5, T1, K1, K2tog, K3, T1, K3, K2tog, K2, T1, K4, K2tog, T1, K5, T1, K2tog, K5, T1, K1, K2tog, K3, T1, K3, K2tog, K1, T1, K5, K2tog, T1, K5, T1, K2tog, K4, T1, K2, K2tog, K3, T1, K3, K2tog, K1, T1, K5, (K2tog and AT THE SAME TIME T1). (88 sts total for hat)

Rnd 6: Knit.

Rnd 7: *K6, K2tog; rep from * to end. Cut B. (77 sts total for hat)

Rnd 8: With A, knit.

Rnd 9: *K5, K2tog; rep from * to end. (66 sts total for hat)

Rnd 10: Using 24" needle and beg at marker, K33. Remove marker. From now on 24" needle marks beg of rnd. Turn and knit across rem 33 sts on 16" needle.

Rnd 11:

Row 1 (24" needle): K4, K2tog, T1, K3, K2tog, K1, T1, K2, K2tog, K2, T1, K1, K2tog, K3, T1, K2tog, K3. Turn. (28 sts)

Row 2 (16" needle): K1, K2tog, T1, K3, K2tog, K1, T1, K2, K2tog, K2, T1, K1, K2tog, K3, T1, K2tog, K4, (K2tog and AT THE SAME TIME T1). Turn. (27 sts)

Rnd 12: Knit.

Rnd 13:

Row 1: (K3, K2tog) 5 times, K2tog, K1. Turn. (22 sts)

Row 2: (K2tog, K3) 5 times, K2. Turn. (22 sts)

Rnd 14: Knit.

Rnd 15:

Row 1: (K2, K2tog) 5 times, K1, sl last st to lockable marker. Turn. (16 sts)

Row 2: Sl st from marker to LH needle, (K2tog, K2) 5 times, K2tog. Turn. (17 sts)

Rnd 16: Knit.

Rnd 17:

Row 1: K1, K2tog, T1, K2tog, K1, K2tog K1, (K2tog and AT THE SAME TIME T1), (K1, K2tog, K1. Turn. (11 sts)

Row 2: (K2tog and AT THE SAME TIME T1), (K1, K2tog) twice, K1, (K2tog and AT THE SAME TIME T1), K1, K2tog, K1, (K2tog and AT THE SAME TIME T1). Turn. (11 sts)

Rnd 18: Knit.

Rnd 19:

Row 1: (K2tog) 5 times, sl last st to lockable marker. Turn. (5 sts)

Row 2: Sl st from marker to LH needle, (K2tog) 6 times. Turn. (6 sts)

Rnd 20: Knit.

Rnd 21:

Row 1: K2tog, K1, K2tog. Turn. (3 sts)

Row 2: (K2tog) 3 times. Turn. (3 sts)

Rnd 22: Knit.

Cut yarn, leaving a 10" tail. Using a tapestry needle, sl tail through rem 6 sts, cinch tight and bring to inside of hat.

Weave in ends.

MITTENS
Cuff

With larger needles and A, CO and set up 39 (39, 45) sts [20 (20, 23) sts on 16" needle; 19 (19, 22) sts on 24" needle]. Follow instructions for "Setting Up the Needles" (page 20).

Setup rnd: Purl.

Inside out, a thrummed mitten looks rather like a Muppet. Right side out, it couldn't be toastier.

Rnd 1:

Row 1 (16" needle): **RM:** RT 3 times, (P1, K1) 3 (3, 4) times, P1, RT 3 times, P1, K0 (0, 1). Rep for **LM.** Turn.

Row 2 (24" needle): **LM:** P0 (0, 1), (K1, P1) 3 times, RT 3 times, (P1, K1) 3 (3, 4) times, P1. Rep for **RM.** Turn.

Rnd 2:

Row 1: **RM:** K6, (P1, K1) 3 (3, 4) times, P1, K6, P1, K0 (0, 1). Rep for **LM.** Turn.

Row 2: **LM:** P0 (0, 1), (K1, P1) 3 times, K6, (P1, K1) 3 (3, 4) times, P1. Rep for **RM.** Turn.

Rnd 3:

Row 1: **RM:** K1, RT twice, (K1, P1) 4 (4, 5) times, K1, RT twice, K1, P1, K0 (0, 1). Rep for **LM.** Turn.

Row 2: **LM:** P0 (0, 1), (K1, P1) 3 times, K1, RT twice, (K1, P1) 4 (4, 5) times. Rep for **RM.** Turn.

Rnd 4: Rep rnd 2.

Work rnds 1–4 another 4 (5, 5) times. Cuff measures approx 2¼ (2¾, 2¾)" from CO edge.

Do not cut A.

Rnd 5: With B, purl.

Rnd 6: Knit. Cut B.

Rnd 7: With A, purl.

Before continuing, attach a lockable marker to the RM cuff on 16" needle for later use.

Small

Rnd 8:

Row 1: **RM:** Knit. **LM:** K6 and put on waste yarn, knit to end. Turn. (20 sts per half, including sts on waste yarn)

Row 2: LM: K6 and put on waste yarn, knit to last st, K1f&b. Sl sts from waste yarn to LH needle, K6. **RM:** Knit to last st, K1f&b. Turn. (20 sts per half, including sts on waste yarn)

Medium

Rnd 8:

Row 1: RM: K5, K1f&b, K9, K1f&b, K4. **LM:** K6 and put on waste yarn, K1f&b, K8, K1f&b, K4. Turn. (22 sts per half, including sts on waste yarn)

Row 2: LM: K6 and put on waste yarn, K1f&b, (K3, K1f&b) twice, K4. Sl sts from waste yarn to LH needle, K6. **RM:** (K4, K1f&b) 3 times, K4. Turn. (22 sts per half, including sts on waste yarn)

Large

Rnd 8:

Row 1: RM: K10, K2tog, knit to end. **LM:** K6 and put on waste yarn, K4, K2tog, knit to end. Turn. (22 sts per half, including sts on waste yarn)

Row 2: LM: K6 and put on waste yarn, knit to end. Sl sts from waste yarn to LH needle, K6. **RM:** Knit. Turn. (22 sts per half, including sts on waste yarn)

Body

All Sizes

(6 sts rem on waste yarn)

Rnd 1:

Row 1: RM: (K3, T1) 5 times, K0 (2, 2). **LM:** (K3, T1) 3 (4, 4) times, K2 (0, 0), sl sts from waste yarn to LH needle, K1 (3, 3), T1, K3 (2, 2), T1 (0, 0). Turn.

Row 2: LM: K3 (1, 1), T1, (K3, T1) 4 (5, 5) times. Rep for **RM.** Turn.

[40 (44, 44) sts total per mitten]

Rnd 2: Knit.

Remember to always knit thrum and regular st tog tbl.

Thumb Gusset

Rnd 1:

Row 1: RM: K1, M1R, K1, M1L, knit to end. Rep for **LM.** Turn. [22 (24, 24) sts per half]

Row 2: Knit. Turn.

Rnd 2: Knit.

Rnd 3:

Row 1: RM: K2, T1, K2, T1, (K3, T1) 4 times, K0 (2, 2). Rep for **LM.** Turn.

Row 2: LM: K3 (1, 1), T1, (K3, T1) 4 (5, 5) times. Rep for **RM.** Turn.

Rnd 4:

Row 1: RM: K1, M1R, K3, M1L, knit to end. Rep for **LM.** Turn. [24 (26, 26) sts per half]

Row 2: Knit. Turn.

Rnd 5: Knit. Cut A.

Rnd 6: With B, knit.

Rnd 7:

Row 1: RM: K1, M1R, K2, T1, K2, M1L, K1, T1, (K3, T1) 4 times, K0 (2, 2). Rep for **LM.** Turn. [26 (28, 28) sts per half]

Row 2: LM: K3 (1, 1), T1, (K3, T1) 4 (5, 5) times. Rep for **RM.** Turn.

Rnds 8 and 9: Knit.

Rnd 10:

Row 1: RM: K1, M1R, K7, M1L, knit to end. Rep for **LM.** Turn. [28 (30, 30) sts per half]

Row 2: Knit. Turn.

Rnd 11:

Row 1: **RM:** (K2, T1) 4 times, (K3, T1) 4 times, K0 (2, 2). Rep for **LM**. Turn.

Row 2: **LM:** K3 (1, 1), T1, (K3, T1) 4 (5, 5) times. Rep for **RM**. Turn.

Rnd 12: Knit.

Small

Rnd 13: Knit.

Rnd 14:

Row 1: **RM:** Sl 11 sts to waste yarn and using backward loop cast on (page 11), CO 3 sts to RH needle tip, knit to end. Rep for **LM**. Turn. (20 sts per half)

Row 2: Knit. Turn. (20 sts per half)

Medium and Large

Rnd 13:

Row 1: **RM:** K1, M1R, K9, M1L, knit to end. Rep for **LM**. Turn. (32 sts per half)

Row 2: Knit. Turn.

Rnd 14: Knit.

Rnd 15:

Row 1: **RM:** K3, T1, (K2, T1) twice, (K3, T1) 5 times, K2. Rep for **LM**. Turn.

Row 2: **LM:** K1, T1, (K3, T1) 5 times. Rep for **RM**. Turn.

Rnds 16 and 17: Knit.

Rnd 18:

Row 1: **RM:** Sl 13 sts to waste yarn and using backward loop cast on, CO 3 sts to RH needle tip, knit to end. Rep for **LM**. Turn. (22 sts per half)

Row 2: Knit. Turn. (22 sts per half)

Mittens measure approx 5 (6, 6)" from CO edge.

Small

Next rnd: *(K3, T1); rep from * to end.

Knit even for 3 rnds.

All Sizes

Rnd 1:

Row 1: **RM:** (K3, T1) 5 times, K0 (2, 2). Rep for **LM**. Turn.

Row 2: **LM:** K3 (1, 1), T1, (K3, T1) 4 (5, 5) times. Rep for **RM**. Turn.

Rnd 2: Knit. Do not cut B.

Rnds 3 and 4: With A, knit.

Rnd 5:

Row 1: **RM:** (K3, T1) 5 times, K0 (2, 2). Rep for **LM**. Turn.

Row 2: **LM:** K3 (1, 1), T1, (K3, T1) 4 (5, 5) times. Rep for **RM**. Turn.

Rnds 6 and 7: Knit. Do not cut A.

Rnd 8: With B, knit.

Rnd 9: Rep rnd 4.

Rnd 10: Knit. Do not cut B.

Rnds 11 and 12: With A, knit.

Rnd 13: Rep rnd 4.

Rnds 14 and 15: Knit.

Rnd 16: With B, knit.

Rnd 17: Rep rnd 4.

Rnds 18–20: Knit.

Rnd 21: Rep rnd 4.

Rnd 22: Knit.

Medium and Large

Knit even for 2 rnds.

Next rnd:

Row 1: RM: (K3, T1) 5 times, K2. Rep for **LM**. Turn.

Row 2: LM: K1, T1, (K3, T1) 5 times. Rep for **RM**. Turn.

Knit 1 rnd.

Crown

All Sizes

Mittens measure approx 8½ (9¼, 9¼)" from CO edge.

Rnd 1:

Row 1: RM: (K3, ssk) once, (K3, K2tog) 3 times, K0 (2, 2). Rep for **LM**. Turn. [16 (18, 18) sts per half]

Row 2: LM: K3 (1, 1), ssk, (K3, K2tog) 3 times, K0 (2, 2), K2tog (0, 1, 1) times. Rep for **RM**. Turn. [16 (17, 17) sts per half]

Rnd 2: Knit.

Rnd 3:

Row 1: RM: (K3, T1) once, (K2, T1) 4 times, K0 (2, 2). Rep for **LM**. Turn.

Row 2: LM: K3 (1, 1), T1, (K2, T1) 4 (5, 5) times. Rep for **RM**. Turn.

Rnd 4: Knit.

Rnd 5:

Row 1: RM: (K2, K2tog) 4 times, K0 (2, 2). Rep for **LM**. Turn. [12 (14, 14) sts per half]

Row 2: LM: K1, ssk, (K2, K2tog) 3 times, K1 (2, 2). Rep for **RM**. Turn. [12 (13, 13) sts per half]

Rnd 6: Knit.

Rnd 7:

Small

Row 1: RM: K2, T1, K1, T1, K2, T1, (K1, T1) twice. Rep for **LM**. Turn.

Row 2: LM: K2, T1, K1, T1, K2, T1, (K1, T1) twice. Rep for **RM**. Turn.

Medium and Large

Row 1: RM: (K2, T1) 2 times, (K1, T1) 3 times, K2. Rep for **LM**. Turn.

Row 2: LM: (K1, T1) 4 times, K2, T1, K1, T1. Rep for **RM**. Turn.

All Sizes

Rnd 8: Knit.

Rnd 9:

Row 1: RM: (K1, K2tog) 4 times, K0 (1, 1), **Medium and Large only:** Sl last st to lockable marker. **All Sizes:** Rep for **LM**. Turn. [8 (9, 9) sts per half]

Row 2: LM: Medium and Large only: Sl 1 st from marker to LH needle. **All Sizes:** (K1, K2tog) 4 times, K0 (K2tog, K2tog). Rep for **RM**. Turn. [8 (9, 9) sts per half]

Rnd 10:

Row 1: RM: (K2tog) 4 times, K0 (1, 1). Rep for **LM**. Turn. [4 (5, 5) sts per half]

Row 2: LM: (K2tog) 4 times, K0 (1, 1). Rep for **RM**. Turn. [4 (5, 5) sts per half]

Cut yarn, leaving a 10" tail. With tapestry needle sl tail through 4 (5, 5) sts of **RM** on 16" needle. Rep for **LM**. Turn. Cont to sl needle through 4 (5, 5) sts of **LM** on 24" needle. Cinch tail tight and pull through to WS. Rep for **RM**.

Thumb

Setup

RM: With thumb gusset on right and marker facing, sl 6 sts from waste yarn to 16" needle, beg at thumb gusset and working toward mitten body. **LM:** With thumb gusset on right and cont with same needle tip, sl 6 sts from waste yarn to 16" needle, beg at thumb gusset and working toward mitten body. Turn.

LM: With thumb gusset on left side, sl rem 5 (7, 7) sts from waste yarn to 24" needle. Cont with same needle tip and rep for **RM**. Turn.

[11 (13, 13) sts total per thumb]

Connect mittens in the middle right above cuff with a lockable st marker or small piece of waste yarn to keep them close together as you knit; slip them behind cables each time you turn work to keep them out of the way of your needles.

Rnd 1:

Row 1 (16" needle): RM: With A, K6, PU 2 (3, 3) sts across CO edge. Rep for **LM**. Turn. [8 (9, 9) sts per half]

Row 2 (24" needle): LM: With RH needle tip, PU 2 (1, 1) sts across CO edge, K7. Rep for **RM**. Turn. [7 (8, 8) sts per half]

[15 (17, 17) sts total per thumb]

Small

Rnds 2 and 3: Knit.

Medium and Large

Rnd 2:

Row 1: RM: (K2, T1) twice, K3. Rep for **LM**. Turn.

Row 2: LM: K1, T1, (K2, T1) twice. Rep for **LM**. Turn.

Rnd 3: Knit.

All Sizes

Rnds 4 and 5: Knit.

Work rnds 2–5 twice more, then rnds 2 and 3 once more.

Dec rnd:

Small

Row 1: RM: (K2, K2tog) twice. Rep for **LM**. Turn. (6 sts per half)

Row 2: LM: K3, K2tog, K2. Rep for **RM**. Turn. (6 sts per half)

Medium and Large

Row 1: RM: (K1, K2tog) 3 times. Rep for **LM**. Turn. (6 sts per half)

Row 2: LM: (K2, K2tog) twice. Rep for RM. Turn. (6 sts per half)

Next rnd: Knit.

Dec rnd: K2tog across. (6 sts total per thumb)

Cut yarn, leaving a 10" tail. Using tapestry needle, sl tail through rem sts of **RM**, change tapestry needle to tail for **LM** and rep. Turn and sl needle through rem sts for **LM**. Cinch tight and bring to inside of mitten. Rep for **RM**. Weave in ends.

flake set

Originally, only the scarf in this three-piece set was to have pom-poms. In my quest for the perfect pom-pom, I tried a pom-pom maker, but the resulting pom-pom was too small for the scarf. After cutting a cardboard template to size and getting the pom-poms I needed, I found myself looking longingly at the lonely, too-small pom-pom and ended up attaching it to the hat. I loved it! Now, with a full-blown case of pom-pom fever, I cut a smaller template and made tiny pom-poms for the mittens as well. The cuteness of it all was utterly stunning. I kept putting the pieces on, turning them this way and that to admire them. Now that I'm a pom-pom–making pro, future projects beware!

Skill level: Intermediate ■■■□

Hat sizes: Women's Small (Medium/Large)

To fit head circumference up to: 20 (22)"

Finished scarf measurements: Approx 6" x 56", excluding pom-poms

Mitten sizes: Women's Small (Medium, Large)

To fit hand circumference up to: 6¾ (7¼, 7¾)"

MATERIALS

Lush from Classic Elite Yarns (50% angora from angora rabbits, 50% wool; 1.75 oz/50 g; 124 yds/113 m) (4)

A 5 skeins in color 4416 Natural

B 3 skeins in color 4420 Aqua Foam

C 2 balls Maggi's Angora from MaggiKnits (90% angora, 10% polyamide; approx 0.9 oz/25 g; 91 yds/82 m) in color 06 Pink (4)

2 size 6 (4 mm) circular needles (16" and 24") or size-required to obtain gauge

2 size 8 (5 mm) circular needles (16" and 24") or size required to obtain gauge

2 size 6 (4 mm) straight needles and 2 size 6 (4 mm) double-pointed needles

Size F-5 (3.75 mm) crochet hook

Cable needle

Point protectors

2 regular and 2 lockable stitch markers

Tapestry needle

Small amount of waste yarn

Cardboard templates for 1", 3", and 4" pom-poms (see instructions on page 66)

GAUGE

5½ sts = 1" in St st using smaller needles

5 sts = 1" in St st using larger needles

SPECIAL INSTRUCTIONS
Making Pom-poms

1. Cut out two circles of cardboard, with a smaller circle cut out of the center and a notch cut out of the resulting ring. Note that the width of the ring must match half the desired diameter of the pom-pom (e.g., for the 3" pom-pom, the ring must measure 1½" from the inner edge to the outer edge).

2. Sandwich the tail of yarn you are using for the pom-pom between the two cardboard layers and begin to wind yarn around the semicircle; the more yarn you use, the fluffier your pom-pom will be.

3. Loosely tie the ends of sandwiched yarn together (it'll be easier to cinch it tight, later). Hold the pom-pom maker tightly in one hand and carefully begin to cut strands of yarn where they pass over the outside edge of the cardboard shape.

4. When you've cut through them, lay the shape on a table and tighten the single knot of sandwiched yarn. Once it's as tight as it can be, knot it again to secure it in place.

5. Pull the cardboard pieces away from the pom-pom and fluff.

Color Work

See "Fair Isle" on page 15, "Snowflake Chart for Hat and Scarf" on page 72, and "Snowflake Chart for Duplicate Stitch on Mitten" on page 72.

K1B (Knit 1 below): K1 in the center of the st below the next st on the LH needle. After knitting in the st below, slip the st off the LH needle. Doing this helps prevent a jog in the pattern when you start a new round.

3/3 LC: Sl 3 sts to cn and hold in front, K3, K3 from cn.

3/3 RC: Sl 3 sts to cn and hold in back, K3, K3 from cn.

HAT

With smaller 16" circular needle and A, CO 100 (110) sts, pm, and being careful not to twist, close rnd.

Knit 5 rnds, then change to larger 16" needle. Beg color work as follows:

Rnd 1: *With A, K3, with C, K2; rep from * to end.

Rnd 2: *With A, K3, with C, P2; rep from * to end.

Rep rnd 2 twice more. Cut C.

Rnds 5–7: Cont with A, knit. Do not cut A.

Rnd 8: With B, knit.

Rnd 9: K1B, knit to end.

Rnd 10: *With A, K1, with B, K1; rep from * to end.

Rnd 11: *With B, K1, with A, K1; rep from * to end.

Rnds 12 and 13: With B, knit. Cut B.

Small

Rnd 14: With A, K28, K2tog, K40, K2tog, K28. (98 sts total for hat)

Medium/Large

Rnd 14: With A, K40, M1R, K30, M1R, K40. (112 sts total for hat)

Rnds 15 and 16: Knit. Remember to K1B at beg of rnd 15.

All Sizes

Work Snowflake chart once (see page 72). Cut C.

Cont with A and knit 3 rnds. Do not cut A.

Next rnd: With B, knit.

Next rnd: K1B, knit to end.

Next rnd: *With A, K1, with B, K1; rep from * to end.

Next rnd: *With B, K1, with A, K1; rep from * to end.

Next 2 rnds: With B, knit. Cut B.

Next rnd: Cont with A, knit.

Next rnd: K1B, knit to end.

Knit 3 (4) more rnds.

In order to make your hat fit exactly as you like it, try it on now and adjust knit rnds as needed, allowing 1½" of length for crown shaping.

Crown

Rnd 1: Cont with A, *K5, K2tog; rep from * to end. [84 (96) sts total for hat]

Rnd 2: Knit.

Rnd 3: *K4, K2tog; rep from * to end. [70 (80) sts total for hat]

Rnd 4: Remove marker and knit across first 35 (40) sts with 16" needle as before. Next pull RH needle tip toward you and down so sts slip to cable and needle tip is out of the way. Using 24" needle, beg to knit across rem 35 (40) unworked sts. [35 (40) sts on each needle] 16" needle marks the beg of rnd from now on.

Rnd 5: *With A, K4, with C, K1; rep from * to end. Turn.

Rnd 6:

Row 1 (16" needle): With A, K1, K2tog, (with C, K3, with A, K2tog) 6 (7) times, with C, K2. Turn.

Row 2 (24" needle): With C, K1, (with A, K2tog, with C, K3) 6 (7) times, with A, K2tog, with C, K2. Turn. [56 (64) sts total for hat]

Rnd 7: *With A, K3, with C, K1; rep from * to end.

Do not cut C.

Rnd 8: With A, (K2, K2tog); rep from * to end. [42 (48) sts total for hat]

Rnd 9: *With A, K1, with C, K1; rep from * to end. Cut C.

Rnd 10: Knit.

Rnd 11: *K1, K2tog; rep from * to end. [28 (32) sts total for hat]

Rnd 12: Knit.

Rnd 13: *K2tog; rep from * to end. [14 (16) sts total for hat]

Cut yarn, leaving a 5" tail.

Thread tail onto tapestry needle, then sl needle through all sts on 16" needle; cont with all sts on 24" needle and cinch tight.

Bring tail to inside of hat, then weave in ends. If necessary, block hat into shape. Using all 3 colors held tog, make one 3" pom-pom (page 66) and sew to top of hat.

SCARF

With larger needles and A, CO 60 sts (30 sts per needle). Follow instructions for "Setting Up the Needles" (page 20).

Rnds 1–8: Knit. Cut A.

Rnd 9: *With B, K3, with C, K2; rep from * to end.

Rnds 10–12: *With B, K3, with C, P2; rep from * to end.

Cut C, do not cut B.

Rnds 13–15: With A, knit. Do not cut A.

Rnd 16: With B, knit.

Rnd 17: K1B, knit to end.

Rnd 18: *With A, K1, with B, K1; rep from * to end.

Rnd 19: *With B, K1, with A, K1; rep from * to end. Do not cut A.

Rnds 20 and 21: With B, knit. Cut B.

Rnds 22–24: With A, knit, dec 4 sts evenly around. (56 sts total for scarf)

Work Snowflake chart (page 72) once.

Cont with A, knit even for 3 rnds. Do not cut A.

Rnd 39: With B, knit, inc 4 sts evenly around. (60 sts total for scarf).

Rnd 40: K1B, knit to end.

Rnd 41: *With A, K1, with B, K1; rep from * to end.

Rnd 42: *With B, K1, with A, K1; rep from * to end. Do not cut A.

Rnds 43 and 44: With B, knit. Cut B.

*With A, knit 40 rnds (scarf measures approx 14" from CO edge). Do not cut A.

With C, knit 2 rnds. Cut C.

With A, knit 40 rnds (scarf measures approx 21" from CO edge). Do not cut A.

With B, knit 2 rnds. Cut B.

Rep from * once more. Scarf measures approx 35" from CO edge.

With A, knit 40 rnds (scarf measures approx 42" from CO edge). Do not cut A.

With C, knit 2 rnds. Cut C.

With A, knit 40 rnds (scarf measures approx 49" from CO edge).

Rep rnds 16–44 once. Do not cut B.

Cont with A, knit 3 rnds. Cut A.

Next rnd: *With B, K3, with C, K2; rep from * to end.

Next rnd: *With B, K3, with C, P2; rep from * to end.

Rep last rnd twice more. Cut B and C.

With A knit 8 rnds, then BO all sts.

Finishing

Weave in ends. Block.

Cut two 15" strands of A and thread one onto tapestry needle. Beg at one end of scarf and weave yarn through one strand only of each BO st; then cinch tight and double knot ends of yarn strand to keep in place. Using all 3 colors held tog, make two 4" pom-poms (page 66) and sew to ends of scarf.

MITTENS
Cable Braid

Instructions for cable braid are written for 2 at a time but you can also work them 1 at a time, if that makes you feel more comfortable.

Using straight needles, crochet hook, waste yarn, and "Provisional Cast On" (page 11), CO 20 sts for one braid. Slide sts toward back of needle and rep for next braid.

Using 2 balls of B, beg cable patt.

Row 1 (RS): Knit.

Row 2 (WS) and all even-numbered rows: K1, P18, K1. Rep for next braid.

Row 3: P1, (3/3 RC) 3 times, P1. Rep for next braid.

Row 5: P1, K18, P1. Rep for next braid.

Row 7: P1, K3, (3/3 LC) twice, K3, P1. Rep for next braid.

Row 9: P1, K18, P1. Rep for next braid.

Lock Braids Together

If working both braids at the same time, connect them on RS in the middle with a lockable marker. This will stop them from separating and make it easier for you to remember to work both. After three reps, move marker up about 1" to keep them connected close to needles.

Work rows 2–9 another 5 times; then work rows 2–8 once more. Cable will measure approx 7" for all sizes.

Clip waste yarn of provisional cast on for one braid, and carefully slip live sts onto a size 6 needle (24" circular or dpn), as you unravel waste yarn (page 53). Using either the three-needle bind off (page 16) or the Kitchener stitch (page 17), connect ends of braid in the rnd. Rep for second braid.

With smaller 16" needle, and with B, PU 16 (18, 18) sts along either cable edge of one braid cuff. Cont with same needle tip and new ball of B, rep for second cuff. Turn work and cont across empty cuff edges. Using smaller 24" needle, PU 18 (18, 20) sts for each cuff. Follow instructions for "Setting Up the Needles" (page 20).

Optional: Hook cuffs together in middle with lockable marker to prevent them from separating to opposite ends of needles. [34 (36, 38) sts total per mitten]

Work in K1, P1 ribbing for 4 (5, 5) rnds. Cuff measures approx 2½ (2¾, 2¾)" from CO edge.

Body

Rnds 1 and 2: Knit. Do not cut B.

Rnd 3: With C, knit. Do not cut C.

Rnd 4: With B, rep rnd 2.

Rnd 5: Rep rnd 3. Cut C.

Thumb Gusset

Rnd 1:

Row 1: RM: K1, M1R, K1, M1L, knit to end. Rep for **LM**. Turn. [18 (20, 20) sts per half]

Row 2: Knit. Turn.

Rnds 2 and 3: Knit.

Rnd 4:

Row 1: RM: K1, M1R, K3, M1L, knit to end. Rep for **LM**. Turn. [20 (22, 22) sts per half]

Row 2: Knit. Turn.

Rnds 5 and 6: Knit.

Rnd 7:

Row 1: RM: K1, M1R, K5, M1L, knit to end. Rep for **LM**. Turn. [22 (24, 24) sts per half]

Row 2: Knit. Turn.

Rnds 8 and 9: Knit.

Rnd 10:

Row 1: RM: K1, M1R, K7, M1L, knit to end. Rep for **LM**. Turn. [24 (26, 26) sts per half]

Row 2: Knit. Turn.

Rnds 11 and 12: Knit.

Rnd 13:

Row 1: RM: K1, M1R, K9, M1L, knit to end. Rep for **LM**. Turn. [26 (28, 28) sts per half]

Row 2: Knit. Turn.

Rnds 14 and 15: Knit.

Medium and Large

Rnd 16:

Row 1: RM: K1, M1R, K11, M1L, knit to end. Rep for **LM**. Turn. (30 sts per half)

Row 2: Knit. Turn.

Rnds 17 and 18: Knit.

All Sizes

Next rnd:

Row 1: RM: Sl 13 (15, 15) sts to waste yarn and using backward loop cast on (page 11), CO 3 sts to RH needle tip, knit to end. Rep for **LM**. Turn. [16 (18, 18) sts per half]

Row 2: Knit. Turn. [18 (18, 20) sts per half]

Mittens measure approx 5¾ (6¼, 6¼)" from CO edge.

Knit even until mittens measure 8½ (9, 9¼)" from CO edge.

Crown

Rnd 1:

Small

Row 1: RM: K1, M1R, knit to last st, M1R, K1. Rep for **LM**. Turn. (18 sts per half)

Row 2: Knit. Turn.

Medium

Rows 1 and 2: Knit. Turn.

Large

Row 1: Knit. Turn.

Row 2: LM: K1, K2tog, knit to last 3 sts, K2tog, K1. Rep for **RM**. Turn. (18 sts per half)

All Sizes

[36 sts total per mitten]

Rnd 2: *K4, K2tog; rep from * to end. (30 sts total per mitten)

Rnds 3 and 4: Knit.

Rnd 5: *K3, K2tog; rep from * to end. (24 sts total per mitten)

Rnds 6 and 7: Knit.

Rnd 8: *K2, K2tog; rep from * to end. (18 sts total per mitten)

Rnds 9 and 10: Knit.

Thread tails through rem sts. Bring tails to inside of mittens and weave in ends.

Mittens measure approx 9¾ (10¼, 10½)" from CO edge.

Thumb

Setup

RM: With thumb on right side, sl 6 sts from waste yarn to 16" needle, beg at thumb gusset and working toward mitten body. Cont with same needle tip and rep for **LM**. Turn.

LM: With thumb on left side, sl rem 7 (9, 9) sts from waste yarn to 24" needle. Cont with same needle tip and rep for **RM**. Turn.

[13 (15, 15) sts total per thumb]

Connect mittens with a piece of scrap yarn or a lockable marker right above the cuff to keep them close together as you work. Make sure to slip mittens behind needle cables and out of the way each time you turn your work.

Rnd 1:

Row 1 (16" needle): **RM:** Reattach yarn, K6, PU 2 sts across CO edge. Rep for **LM.** Turn. (8 sts per half)

Sl mittens behind both cables.

Row 2 (24" needle): **LM:** With RH needle tip, PU 1 st across CO edge, K7 (9, 9). Rep for **RM.** Turn. [8 (10, 10) sts per half]

Knit even for 10 (11, 12) rnds.

Thumb Crown

Small

Rnd 1: Knit.

Medium and Large

Rnd 1:

Row 1: Knit.

Row 2: **LM:** K1, K2tog, knit to last 3 sts, K2tog, K1. Rep for **RM.** Turn. (8 sts per half)

All Sizes

Rnd 2: (K2, K2tog) across. (12 sts total per thumb)

Rnd 3: Knit.

Rnd 4: *K2tog across. (6 sts total per thumb)

RM: Thread tail onto tapestry needle, then slip needle through rem sts and cinch tight. Rep for **LM.** Turn and rep for sts on 24" needle.

Bring tails to inside of mittens and weave in ends.

With A and using the duplicate stitch method (page 14), follow the snowflake chart (page 72) to embroider a snowflake on the back of each mitten. Using all 3 colors held tog, make two 1" pom-poms (page 66) and sew to cuffs of mittens.

Snowflake Chart for Hat and Scarf

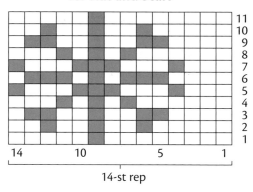

14-st rep

Key

☐ White
▨ Pink

Snowflake Chart for Duplicate Stitch on Mitten

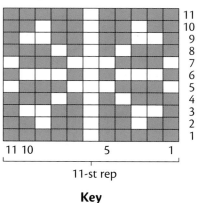

11-st rep

Key

▨ Blue
☐ White

basic gloves

The trick to knitting gloves is: *Take your time.* They're not complicated, just a bit tedious when it comes to the fingers. A yarn with cool variegation and an attractive little cuff pattern will keep you interested until you reach the fingers. And then take it nice and slow; if you get too frustrated, you can put glove stitches on waste yarn (use different-colored yarn for each needle) and work the fingers one at a time. Remember that, above all, you're supposed to enjoy knitting, not despise it.

Skill level: Intermediate ■■■□

Sizes: Women's Small (Medium, Large)

To fit hand circumference up to: 6¾ (7¼, 7¾)"

MATERIALS

2 skeins Vigna from Trendsetter Yarns (52% wool, 48% acrylic; 1.75 oz/50 g; 104 yds/95 m) in color 350 Spanish Sunset (4)

2 size 5 (3.75 mm) circular needles (16" and 24") or size required to obtain gauge

Point protectors

4 regular and 4 lockable stitch markers

Tapestry needle

Small amount of waste yarn

GAUGE

5 sts = 1" in St st

CUFF

CO and set up 32 (36, 40) sts. [16 (16, 20) sts on 16" needle; 16 (20, 20) sts on 24" needle] Follow instructions for "Setting Up the Needles" (page 20).

Rnds 1 and 2: *P2, K2; rep from * to end.

Rnd 3: *P2, (YO, K2, pass YO over K2); rep from * to end.

Rnd 4: *P2, K2; rep from * to end.

Rnd 5: *P2, K1, YO, K1; rep from * to end. [40 (45, 50) sts total per glove]

Rnd 6: *P2, K3; rep from * to end.

Rnd 7: *P2, (sl 1, K2, psso); rep from * to end. [32 (36, 40) sts total per glove]

Rnd 8: *P2, K2; rep from * to end.

Work rnds 5–8 another 2 (3, 3) times. Cuff measures 2 (2¾, 2¾)" from CO edge.

Medium

Shifting rnd:

Row 1 (16" needle): Knit. Turn.

***Row 2 (24" needle):* LG:** K2 and place on lockable marker, knit to end. Rep for **RG.** Turn.

Next rnd:

***Row 1:* RG:** Knit, sl sts from marker to LH needle, K2. Rep for **LG.** Turn. (18 sts per half)

Row 2: Knit. Turn. (18 sts per half)

Large

Dec rnd:

***Row 1:* RG:** K2tog, knit to end. Rep for **LG.** Turn. (19 sts per half)

***Row 2:* LG:** K2tog, knit to end. Rep for **RG.** Turn. (19 sts per half)

All Sizes

[32 (36, 38) sts total per glove]

BODY

Knit even for 5 (3, 4) rnds.

THUMB GUSSET

Place a lockable marker at bottom of cuff of **RG** (first glove to be worked). This marker indicates beg of rnd and helps distinguish between **RG** and **LG.**

From now on, 16" needle carries palm sts and 24" needle carries sts for back of hand.

Rnd 1:

***Row 1 (16" needle):* RG:** K1f&b, K1, K1f&b, knit to end. **LG:** Knit to last 3 sts, pm, K1f&b, K1, K1f&b. Turn. [18 (20, 21) sts per half]

Sl marker as you come to it.

Row 2 (24" needle): Knit. Turn.

Rnds 2 and 3: Knit.

Rnd 4:

***Row 1:* RG:** K1f&b, K3, K1f&b, knit to end. **LG:** Knit to marker, K1f&b, K3, K1f&b. Turn. [20 (22, 23) sts per half]

Row 2: Knit. Turn.

Rnds 5 and 6: Knit.

Rnd 7:

***Row 1:* RG:** K1f&b, K5, K1f&b, knit to end. **LG:** Knit to marker, K1f&b, K5, K1f&b. Turn. [22 (24, 25) sts per half]

Row 2: Knit. Turn.

Rnds 8 and 9: Knit.

Rnd 10:

***Row 1:* RG:** K1f&b, K7, K1f&b, knit to end. **LG:** Knit to marker, K1f&b, K7, K1f&b. Turn. [24 (26, 27) sts per half]

Row 2: Knit. Turn.

Rnds 11 and 12: Knit.

Rnd 13:

***Row 1:* RG:** K1f&b, K9, K1f&b, knit to end. **LG:** Knit to marker, K1f&b, K9, K1f&b. Turn. [26 (28, 29) sts per half]

Row 2: Knit. Turn.

Rnd 14:

For **LG** thumb to be mirror image of **RG** thumb, a couple of sts have to be moved as follows:

***Row 1:* RG:** Knit. **LG:** K1 and sl to lockable marker, knit to end. Turn.

Row 2: LG: K1 and sl to lockable marker, knit to end, sl st from marker to LH needle, K1. **RG:** Knit. Turn.

Rnd 15:

Row 1: RG: Knit. **LG:** Knit, sl st from marker to LH needle, K1. Turn.

Row 2: Knit. Turn.

Rnd 16: Remove markers as you come to them.

Row 1: RG: K1, sl next 12 sts to waste yarn; with backward loop cast on (page 11), CO 2 sts to RH needle to close gap, knit to end. **LG:** Knit to marker, K1, sl next 12 sts to waste yarn, with backward loop cast on CO 2 sts to RH needle to close gap. Turn. [16 (18, 19) sts per half]

Row 2: Knit. Turn. [16 (18, 19) sts per half]

Knit even until gloves measure 3¾ (4, 4½)" from top of cuff.

PINKY

Rnd 1:

Row 1 (16" needle): RG: K12 (14, 14) and sl to waste yarn. Using the cable CO (page 11), CO 2 sts, K6 (6, 7). **LG:** K4 (4, 5), using backward loop cast on, CO 2 sts. Sl rem 12 (14, 14) sts to waste yarn. Turn. [6 (6, 7) sts per half]

Row 2 (24" needle): LG: Sl 12 (13, 14) sts to waste yarn. Using cable cast on, CO 1 st, K5 (6, 6) sts. **RG:** K4 (5, 5), then using backward loop cast on, CO 1 st. Sl 12 (13, 14) sts to waste yarn. Turn. [5 (6, 6) sts per half]

[11 (12, 13) sts total per pinky]

Connect the two gloves with a piece of scrap yarn or a lockable marker right above the cuff to keep them close together as you work. Make sure to slip mittens behind needle cables and out of the way each time you turn your work.

Knit even until pinky measures approx 1¾ (1⅞, 2)" from base.

Dec rnd:

Small

Row 1: RG: *K2tog; rep from * to end. Rep for **LG**. Turn. (3 sts per half)

Row 2: LG: (K2tog) twice, K1. Rep for **RG**. Turn. (3 sts per half)

Medium

Rows 1 and 2: *K2tog; rep from * to end. (6 sts total per pinky)

Large

Row 1: RG: (K2tog) 3 times, K1. Rep for **LG**. Turn. (4 sts per half)

Row 2: LG: *K2tog; rep from * to end. Rep for **RG**. Turn. (3 sts per half)

All Sizes

Cut yarn, leaving 5" tails. Thread through rem sts. Pull tight, closing gap; bring tail to WS and secure.

Next, with palms facing, sl 12 (14, 14) palm sts for **RG** from waste yarn back to 16" needle beg at index finger. Cont with same needle tip and sl 12 (14, 14) palm sts for **LG** from waste yarn back to 16" needle beg at ring finger. Turn.

With backs of hands facing, sl 12 (13, 14) sts for **LG** from waste yarn to 24" needle to beg index finger. Cont with same needle tip and sl 12 (13, 14) sts for **RG** from waste yarn to 24" needle to beg ring finger. Turn.

Inc rnd:

Small

Row 1: RG: Reattach yarn, (K4, M1L) twice, K4, PU 1 st at base of pinky. **LG:** Reattach yarn, then cont with same (RH) needle tip, PU 1 st at base of pinky, (K4, M1L) twice, K4. Turn. (15 sts per half)

Row 2: LG: (K4, M1L) twice, K4, PU 1 st at base of pinky. **RG:** Cont with same (RH) needle tip, PU 1 st at base of pinky, (K4, M1L), K4. Turn. (15 sts per half)

Medium

Row 1: RG: Reattach yarn, (K5, M1L) twice, K4, PU 2 sts at base of pinky. **LG:** Reattach yarn, then cont with same (RH) needle tip, PU 1 st at base of pinky, M1L, (K5, M1L) twice, K4. Turn. (18 sts per half)

Row 2: LG: K4, M1L, (K3, M1L) twice, K3, PU 1 st at base of pinky. **RG:** Cont with same (RH) needle tip, PU 1 st at base of pinky, K4, M1L, (K3, M1L) twice, K3. Turn. (17 sts per half)

Large

Row 1: RG: Reattach yarn, (K5, M1L) twice, K4, PU 2 sts at base of pinky. **LG:** Reattach yarn, then cont with same (RH) needle tip, PU 1 st at base of pinky, K3, M1L, (K4, M1L) twice, K3. Turn. (18 sts per half)

Row 2: LG: K4, (K5, M1L) twice, PU 2 sts at base of pinky. **RG:** Cont with same (RH) needle tip, PU 1 st at base of pinky, K3, M1L, (K4, M1L) twice, K3. Turn. (18 sts per half)

All Sizes

Knit 1 (2, 2) rnds.

RING FINGER

Rnd 1:

Row 1 (16" needle): RG: K9 (11, 11) and sl to waste yarn, K6 (7, 7). **LG:** K6 (6, 7), sl rem sts to waste yarn. Turn.

Row 2 (24" needle): LG: K9 (11, 11) and sl to waste yarn, K6 (7, 7). **RG:** K6 (6, 7), sl rem sts to waste yarn. Turn.

[12 (13, 14) sts total per ring finger]

Knit even until ring finger measures approx 2¼ (2½, 2½)" from base.

Dec rnd:

Small

K2tog across. (6 sts total per ring finger)

Medium

Row 1: RG: (K2tog) 3 times, K1. **LG:** (K2tog) 3 times. Turn.

Row 2: LG: (K2tog) 3 times, K1. **RG:** (K2tog) 3 times. Turn. (7 sts total per ring finger)

Large

*(K2tog) 3 times, K1; rep from * to end. (8 sts total per ring finger)

All Sizes

Finish as for pinky.

With palms (RS) facing, thumb gusset on right, skip 5 (5, 6) sts, then sl next 4 (6, 5) sts for **RG** from waste yarn back to 16" needle. Cont with same needle tip, sl 4 (6, 5) palm sts for **LG** (thumb gusset on left) from waste yarn to 16" needle. Turn.

With backs of hands (RS) facing, skip 4 (6, 5) sts, then sl next 5 (5, 6) sts for **LG** from waste yarn to 24" needle. Cont with same needle tip and sl 5 (5, 6) sts for **RG** from waste yarn to 24" needle. Turn.

MIDDLE FINGER
Rnd 1:

Row 1 (16" needle): **RG:** Reattach yarn, K4 (6, 5), PU 2 (1, 2) sts at base of ring finger. **LG:** Reattach yarn, PU 2 (1, 2) sts at base of ring finger, K4 (6, 5) sts. Turn. [6 (7, 7) sts per half]

Row 2 (24" needle): **LG:** K5 (5, 6), PU 2 sts at base of ring finger. **RG:** PU 2 sts at base of ring finger, K5 (5, 6). Turn. [7 (7, 8) sts per half]

[13 (14, 15) sts total per middle finger]

Knit even until middle finger measures approx 2½ (2¾, 2¾)" from base.

Dec rnd:

Small

Row 1: **RG:** *K2tog; rep from * to end. Rep for **LG**. Turn. (3 sts per half)

Row 2: **LG:** *(K2tog) 3 times, K1. Rep for **RG**. Turn. (4 sts per half)

Medium

*(K2tog) 3 times, K1; rep from * to end. (8 sts total per middle finger)

Large

Row 1: **RG:** (K2tog) 3 times, K1. Rep for **LG**. Turn. (4 sts per half)

Row 2: **LG:** *K2tog; rep from * to end. Rep for **RG**. Turn. (4 sts per half)

All Sizes

[7 (8, 8) sts total for middle finger]

Finish as for pinky.

With palms (RS) facing and thumb gusset on right, sl rem 5 (5, 6) sts for **RG** from waste yarn back to 16" needle. Cont with same needle tip and sl 5 (5, 6) palm sts for **LG** (thumb gusset on left) from waste yarn to 16" needle. Turn.

With backs of hands (RS) facing, sl rem 4 (6, 5) sts for **LG** from waste yarn to 24" needle. Cont with same needle tip and sl rem 4 (6, 5) sts for **RG** from waste yarn to 24" needle. Turn.

INDEX FINGER
Rnd 1:

Row 1 (16" needle): **RG:** Reattach yarn, K5 (5, 6), PU 2 sts at base of middle finger. **LG:** Reattach yarn, PU 2 sts at base of middle finger, K5 (5, 6) sts. Turn. [7 (7, 8) sts per half]

Row 2 (24" needle): **LG:** K4 (6, 5), PU 2 (1, 2) sts at base of middle finger. **RG:** PU 2 (1, 2) sts at base of middle finger, K4 (6, 5). Turn. [6 (7, 7) sts per half]

[13 (14, 15) sts total per index finger]

Knit even until index finger measures approx 2¼ (2½, 2½)" from base.

Dec rnd:

Small

Row 1: **RG:** (K2tog) 3 times, K1. Rep for **LG**. Turn. (4 sts per half)

Row 2: **LG:** (K2tog) 3 times. Rep for **RG**. Turn. (3 sts per half)

Medium

*(K2tog) 3 times, K1; rep from * to end. (8 sts total per index finger)

Large

Row 1: RG: (K2tog) 4 times. Rep for **LG**. Turn. (4 sts per half)

Row 2: LG: (K2tog) 3 times, K1. Rep for **RG**. Turn. (4 sts per half)

All Sizes

[7 (8, 8) sts total for index finger]

Finish as for pinky. Weave in ends.

THUMB

Setup

RG: With thumb gusset on right side and marker facing, sl 6 sts from waste yarn to 16" needle, beg at thumb gusset and working toward mitten body. **LG:** With thumb gusset on left side cont with same needle tip, sl 6 sts from waste yarn to 16" needle, beg at mitten body and working toward thumb gusset. Turn.

LG: With thumb gusset on right side, sl rem 6 sts from waste yarn to 24" needle. Cont with same needle tip and rep for **RG**. Turn.

[12 (12, 12) sts total per thumb]

Next rnd:

Row 1 (16" needle): RG: Reattach yarn, K6, PU 2 (3, 3) sts across CO edge. **Medium only:** Sl last PU st to lockable marker. Rep for **LG**. Turn. [8 (9, 9) sts per half]

Row 2 (24" needle): LG: Medium only: Sl st from marker to RH needle. With RH needle tip, PU 1 (2, 2) st across CO edge, K6. Rep for **RG**. Turn. [7 (8, 8) sts per half]

[15 (17, 17) sts total per thumb]

Knit even until thumb measures approx 1½ (1¾, 2)" from marker.

THUMB CROWN

Small

Row 1: RG: (K2tog) 4 times. Rep for **LG**. Turn. (4 sts per half)

Row 2: LG: (K2tog) 3 times, K1. Rep for **RG**. Turn. (4 sts per half)

Medium and Large

Row 1: RG: (K2tog, K1) 3 times. Rep for **LG**. Turn. (6 sts per half)

Row 2: LG: (K2tog) 4 times. Rep for **RG**. Turn. (4 sts per half)

All Sizes

Cut yarn, leaving a 10" tail. Using tapestry needle, sl tail through rem sts of **RG**, cinch tight, and bring to WS. Rep for **LG**.

Weave in ends.

bobblelicious

In the beginning, I had ideas. I had visions, and I had many colorful skeins of the lovely Gems from Louet North America. Then I cast on and began to knit, and as the needles clicked away, quite suddenly I realized that I had become the tool and my glorious gloves guided my hands into their own creation.

Skill level: Experienced ◼◼◼◼

Sizes: Women's Small (Medium, Large)

To fit hand circumference up to: 6¾ (7¼, 7¾)"

MATERIALS

Gems Merino Fingering Weight from Louet North America (100% merino wool; 1.75 oz/50 g; 185 yds/170 m) ⓵

A 1 skein in color 55 Willow

B 1 skein in color 54 Teal

C 1 skein in color 63 Candy Apple Red

D 1 skein in color 64 Dusty Rose

E 1 skein in color 45 Violet

F 1 skein in color 26 Crabapple Blossom

G 1 skein in color 70 Pure White

2 size 1.5 (2.5 mm) circular needles (16" and 24") or size required to obtain gauge

2 size 1.5 (2.5 mm) double-pointed needles

4 buttons to fit I-cord loops: 2 approx ¾" diameter and 2 approx ½" diameter

Approx 30 size 6/0 glass beads

Size 13 (0.85 mm) steel crochet hook

Point protectors

2 regular and 4 lockable stitch markers

Tapestry needle

Small amount of waste yarn

GAUGE

7¼ sts = 1" in St st

SPECIAL INSTRUCTIONS

Garter st in the rnd: Alternately purl 1 row, knit 1 row.

MB (bobble): (K1, P1, K1, P1, K1) all in 1 st, turn, P5, turn, K5, turn, P5, turn. Skip over first st (closest to needle tip) and sl next 4 sts over it and off LH needle one at a time. 1 st rem, K1tbl.

MBB (beaded bobble): (K1, P1, K1, P1, K1) all in 1 st, turn, P5, turn, K5, turn, P2, place bead on crochet hook in RH, sl st to be beaded from left needle to hook, it will now sit in front of bead. With LH thumb and index finger pinch st tightly and carefully pull it through bead. Sl beaded st back to left needle, purl it and rem sts of bobble as usual. Turn, then skip over first st (closest to needle tip) and sl next 4 sts over it and off LH needle one at a time. 1 st rem, K1tbl.

Color Work: Refer to "Fair Isle" on page 15 and follow the charted patterns on page 93 as called for in glove instructions.

CUFF

With A, CO and set up 60 sts (31 sts on 16" needle and 29 sts on 24" needle) for each glove. Follow instructions for "Setting Up the Needles" (page 20).

Rnds 1–10: Work bobble patt (chart A on page 92) once.

Rnd 11: Knit. Cut yarn.

Rnd 12: With B, knit.

Rnds 13–22: Work rnds 1–10 of bobble patt.

Rnd 23: Knit. Cut yarn.

Rnd 24: With C, knit.

Rnd 25: Work rnd 1 of bobble patt as follows:

Row 1 (16" needle): **RG:** P2, (MBB, P3) 7 times, MBB. Rep for **LG**. Turn.

Row 2 (24" needle): **LG:** (P3, MBB) 7 times, P1. Rep for **RG**. Turn.

Rnds 26–34: Work rnds 2–10 of bobble patt.

Dec rnd:

Small

Row 1: **RG:** With C, (P2, K1, K2tog) twice, P2, K2tog, K1, P1, P2tog, (K2, P2tog, P1) twice, K2, sl rem st on lockable marker. Rep for **LG**. Turn. (24 sts per half)

Row 2: **LG:** Sl st from marker to LH needle, (P2, K1, K2tog) twice, P2, K2tog, K1, P1, P2tog, (K2, P2tog, P1) twice, K2. Rep for **RG**. Turn. (24 sts per half)

Medium

Row 1: **RG:** With C, (P2, K2, P1, P2tog, K2, P2, K1, K2tog) twice, P2, sl rem st on lockable marker. Rep for **LG**. Turn. (26 sts per half)

Row 2: **LG:** Sl st from marker to LH needle, (K2, P2, K1, K2tog, P2, K2, P1, P2tog) twice, K2. Rep for **RG**. Turn. (26 sts per half)

Large

Row 1: **RG:** With C, (P2, K2) twice, P1, P2tog, (K2, P2) twice, K1, K2tog, (P2, K2) twice, sl rem st on lockable marker. Rep for **LG**. Turn. (28 sts per half)

Row 2: **LG:** Sl st from marker to LH needle, (P2, K2) twice, P1, P2tog, (K2, P2) twice, K1, K2tog, (P2, K2) twice. Rep for **RG**. Turn. (28 sts per half)

All Sizes

[48 (52, 56) sts total per glove]

Work in P2, K2 ribbing until ribbing measures ½ (¾, ¾)".

Fair Isle Rib

Work in P2, K2 ribbing. See "Fair Isle" on page 15. On rnds 1, 3, and 5, move C to front to P2, then pass C to back between needles and with D, K2.

Rnds 1, 3, and 5:

Row 1: **RG:** *With C, P2, with D, K2; rep from * to end. Rep with **LG**. Turn.

Row 2: **LG:** *With C, P2, with D, K2; rep from * to end. Rep with **RG**. Turn.

Rnds 2, 4, and 6: Work K2, P2 ribbing with C only, but do not cut D. Instead pull it up (not too tightly!) on inside of glove, ready to be used in the Fair Isle patt of next rnd.

After rnd 6 is completed, cut D. Rep rnd 6 once more. Cut C.

BODY

Connect gloves right above cuff with a piece of scrap yarn or a lockable marker to keep them close together as you work thumbs and fingers. Make sure to keep needle cables in front of gloves by slipping gloves behind them and out of the way each time you turn your work.

With E, knit even for 3 (4, 4) rnds.

THUMB GUSSET

From now on, the 16" needle carries the palm sts and the 24" needle carries the sts for back of hand.

Rnd 1:

Row 1 (16" needle): **RG:** With A, K1f&b, K1, K1f&b, pm, knit to end. **LG:** Knit to last 3 sts, pm, K1f&b, K1, K1f&b. Turn. [26 (28, 30) sts per half]

Sl markers as you come to them.

Row 2 (24" needle): Knit. Turn.

Rnd 2: *With E, K1, with A, K1; rep from * to end.

Rnd 3: With A knit. Cut A, cont with E.

Rnd 4:

Row 1: **RG:** K1f&b, K3, K1f&b, knit to end. **LG:** Knit to marker, K1f&b, K3, K1f&b. Turn. [28 (30, 32) sts per half]

Row 2: Knit. Turn.

Rnds 5 and 6: Knit.

Rnd 7:

Row 1: **RG:** K1f&b, K5, K1f&b, knit to end. **LG:** Knit to marker, K1f&b, K5, K1f&b. Turn. [30 (32, 34) sts per half]

Row 2: Knit. Turn.

Rnd 8: *With F, K1, with E, K1; rep from * to end.

Cut E and cont with F.

Rnd 9: Knit.

Rnd 10:

Row 1: **RG:** K1f&b, K7, K1f&b, knit to end. **LG:** Knit to marker, K1f&b, K7, K1f&b. Turn. [32 (34, 36) sts per half]

Row 2: Knit. Turn.

Rnds 11 and 12: Knit.

Rnd 13:

Row 1: **RG:** K1f&b, K9, K1f&b, knit to end. **LG:** Knit to marker, K1f&b, K9, K1f&b. Turn. [34 (36, 38) sts per half]

Row 2: Knit. Turn.

Rnd 14: With F, knit. Do not cut F.

Rnd 15: With B, knit.

Rnd 16:

Row 1: **RG:** K1f&b, K11, K1f&b, knit to end. **LG:** Knit to marker, K1f&b, K11, K1f&b. Turn. [36 (38, 40) sts per half]

Row 2: Knit. Cut B. Turn.

Rnd 17: With F, knit. Do not cut F.

Rnd 18: With D, knit.

Rnd 19:

Row 1: **RG:** K1f&b, K13, K1f&b, knit to end. **LG:** Knit to marker, K1f&b, K13, K1f&b. Turn. [38 (40, 42) sts per half]

Row 2: Knit. Cut D. Turn.

Rnds 20 and 21: With F, knit.

Rnd 22:

Remove markers as you come to them.

Row 1: RG: K1, sl next 15 sts to waste yarn; with backward loop cast on (page 11) CO 2 sts to RH needle to close gap. Knit to end. **LG:** Knit to marker, K1, sl next 15 sts to waste yarn, with backward loop cast on, CO 2 sts to RH needle to close gap, K1. Turn. [25 (27, 29) sts per half]

Row 2: Knit. Turn. [24 (26, 28) sts per half]

Inc rnd:

Small

Row 1: RG: K7, M1L, (K6, M1L) twice, K6. Rep for **LG.** Turn. (28 sts per half)

Row 2: LG: (K5, M1L) 4 times, K4. Rep for **RG.** Turn. (28 sts per half)

Medium

Row 1: RG: (K7, M1L) 3 times, K6. Rep for **LG.** Turn. (30 sts per half)

Row 2: LG: K4, M1L, (K6, M1L) 3 times, K4. Rep for **RG.** Turn. (30 sts per half)

Large

Row 1: RG: K7, M1L, (K8, M1L) twice, K6. Rep for **LG.** Turn. (32 sts per half)

Row 2: LG: K6, M1L, (K5, M1L) 3 times, K7. Rep for **RG.** Turn. (32 sts per half)

[56 (60, 64) sts total per glove]

All Sizes

With B and F, work rnds 1–6 of chart B (page 93). Each rnd will be worked twice per needle, once for each glove, a total of 4 repeats.

Avoiding Long Floats

On several rounds of chart B, color strands are carried across as much as five stitches. To avoid long "floats" that can get caught on jewelry or fingernails, twist strands after working two or three stitches throughout the chart.

GLOVE HOODIE SETUP

Rnd 7 of Chart B:

Row 1 (16" needle): Knit in color patt. Turn.

Row 2 (24" needle): LG: *With F, knit into shoulder of st below as if to LIR but do not knit corresponding st on LH neeedle; instead sl it pw to RH needle. With B, knit into shoulder of st below as if to LIR but do not knit corresponding st on LH needle; instead sl it pw to RH needle; rep from * to end, ending with a sl st in F. Rep for **RG.** [56 (60, 64) sts total per hoodie]

Important

Do not accidentally knit the stitches that have to be slipped. You'll end up having to undo row 2 completely and start over . . . grrrr, I had to!

Rnd 8 of Chart B:

Row 1: Work in color patt to end. Turn.

Row 2: LG: Hold 2 dpn parallel to each other in right hand. Work across 24" needle, alternately slipping inc sts to back dpn and sl st to front dpn. [28 (30, 32) sts per dpn]

Sl sts pw from front dpn to waste yarn. With 24" needle, work rnd 8 of chart B. Work rnds 9 and 10 of chart B. Cut F. Rep for **RG.** Turn.

Dec rnd:

Small

Rows 1 and 2: With B, knit. (28 sts per half)

Medium

Row 1: RG: With B, (K9, K2tog) twice, K8. Rep for **LG**. Turn. (28 sts per half)

Row 2: LG: With B, (K9, K2tog) twice, K2, sl rem 6 sts unknit from LH to RH needle. **RG:** (K9, K2tog) twice, K8. Turn. (28 sts per half)

Large

Row 1: RG: (K9, K2tog) twice, K10. Rep for **LG**. Turn. (30 sts per half)

Row 2: LG: (K9, K2tog) twice, K3, sl rem 7 sts from LH to RH needle. **RG:** (K9, K2tog) twice, K10. Turn. (30 sts per half)

All Sizes

[56 (56, 60) sts total per glove]

Hand measures approx 3¼ (3½, 3¾)" from top of ribbing. Do not cut B.

PINKY

Rnd 1:

Row 1 (16" needle): RG: Sl 22 (22, 23) sts to waste yarn. With G and using cable CO method (page 11), CO 2 (2, 1) sts, then K8. **LG:** With G, K6 (6, 7) then using the backward loop method, CO 2 (2, 1) sts. Sl rem 22 (22, 23) sts to waste yarn. Turn. [8 sts per half]

Row 2 (24" needle): LG: Sl 22 (22, 23) sts to waste yarn. Cont with G and using cable CO method, CO 1, then K7 (7, 8) sts. **RG:** Cont with G, K6 (6, 7) sts, then using the backward loop method, CO 1 st. Sl rem 22

(22, 23) sts to waste yarn. Turn. [7 (7, 8) sts per half]

[15 (15, 16) sts total per pinky]

Rnds 2 and 3: Knit. Cut G.

With C, knit 5 (5, 6) rnds.

Beg with a purl row, work in garter st for 6 rnds.

Last rnd:

Row 1: RG: BO kw, put last st on lockable marker. Rep for **LG**. Turn.

Row 2: LG: Sl stitch from marker to RH needle and cont BO kw across all sts. Rep for **RG**. Turn. Cut C.

RING FINGER

With palms facing, sl glove sts from waste yarn back to needles as follows:

Sl all palm sts for **RG** to 16" needle beg at index finger. Cont with same needle tip and sl all palm sts for **LG** to 16" needle beg at ring finger. Turn.

With backs of hands facing, sl all sts for **LG** to 24" needle beg at index finger. Cont with same needle tip and sl all sts for **RG** to 24" needle beg at ring finger. Turn.

Rnd 1:

Palms are facing. Cont with B.

Row 1 (16" needle): RG: Knit to end, PU 1 st at base of pinky. **LG:** PU 1 st at base of pinky, knit to end. Turn. [23 (23, 24) sts per half]

Row 2 (24" needle): LG: Knit to end, PU 1 st at base of pinky. **RG:** PU 1 st at base of pinky then knit to end. Turn. [23 (23, 24) sts per half]

[46 (46, 48) sts total per glove]

Rnds 2–4: Knit. Cut B.

Rnd 5:

Row 1: **RG:** Sl 15 (15, 16) sts to waste yarn. Cont with A, K8. **LG:** With A K8, sl rem 15 (15, 16) sts to waste yarn. Turn. (8 sts per half)

Row 2: **LG:** Sl 15 sts to waste yarn, K8 (8, 9). **RG:** K8 (8, 9), sl rem 15 sts to waste yarn. Turn. [8 (8, 9) sts per half]

[16 (16, 17) sts per ring finger]

Knit 5 rnds. Do not cut A.

Next rnd: With E, knit. Do not cut yarn. Twist A over E.

Next rnd: With A, knit. Twist E over A.

Work last 2 rnds twice more. Cut A.

With E and beg with purl row, work garter st for 6 rnds.

Last rnd: BO as for pinky. Turn. Cut E.

MIDDLE FINGER

With palms facing, sl glove sts from waste yarn back to needles as follows:

Sl all palm sts for **RG** to 16" needle beg at index finger. Cont with same needle tip and sl all palm sts for **LG** to 16" needle beg at ring finger. Turn.

With backs of hands facing, sl all sts for **LG** to 24" needle beg at index finger. Cont with same needle tip and sl all sts for **RG** to 24" needle beg at ring finger. Turn.

Rnd 1:

Row 1 (16" needle): **RG:** Sl 8 sts to waste yarn. Cont with D, K7 (7, 8), PU 1 st at base of ring finger. **LG:** With A, PU 1 st at base of ring finger, K7 (7, 8), sl rem 8 sts to waste yarn. Turn. [8 (8, 9) sts per half]

Row 2 (24" needle): **LG:** Sl 7 (7, 8) sts to waste yarn, K8, PU 1 st at base of ring finger. **RG:** PU 1 st at base of ring finger, K8, sl rem 7 (7, 8) sts to waste yarn. (9 sts per half)

[17 (17, 18) sts total per middle finger]

Rnds 2–5: Knit. Do not cut D.

Rnd 6: With G, knit. Do not cut yarn. Twist D over G.

Rnd 7: With D, knit. Twist G over D.

Work rnds 6 and 7 twice more. Cut G.

Cont with D, knit 4 rnds.

Beg with a purl row, work in garter st for 6 rnds.

Last rnd: BO as for pinky. Turn. Cut D.

INDEX FINGER

With palms facing, sl rem sts for **RG** to 16" needle. Cont with same needle tip and sl rem palm sts for **LG** to 16" needle. Turn.

With backs of hands facing, sl rem sts for **LG** to 24" needle and cont with same needle tip sl rem sts for **RG** to 24" needle. Turn.

Rnd 1:

Row 1 (16" needle): **RG:** With F, K8, PU 1 st at base of middle finger. **LG:** With F, PU 1 st at base of middle finger, K8. Turn.

(9 sts per half)

Row 2 (24" needle): **LG:** K7 (7, 8), PU 1 st at base of middle finger. **RG:** PU 1 st at base of middle finger, K7 (7, 8). Turn. [8 (8, 9) sts per half]

[17 (17, 18) sts total per index finger]

Rnds 2–5: Knit. Do not cut F.

Rnd 6: With A, knit. Do not cut yarn. Twist F over A.

Rnd 7: With F, knit. Twist A over F.

Work rnds 6 and 7 twice more. Cut A.

With F, knit 4 rnds.

Beg with a purl row, work 6 rnds garter st.

Last rnd: BO as for pinky. Turn. Cut F.

> ### Tip
> To get rid of some clutter, take a moment and weave in your ends before continuing with thumbs and glove hoodies.

THUMB

RG: With palm facing, sl 7 sts from waste yarn to 16" needle, beg at thumb gusset and working toward glove body. **LG:** Cont with same needle tip and sl 7 sts from waste yarn to 16" needle, beg at mitten body. Turn.

LG: With backs of hands facing, sl rem 8 sts from waste yarn to 24" needle. Rep for **RG**. Turn.

Rnd 1:

Row 1 (16" needle): **RG:** With E, K7. Using a dpn, PU 8 (8, 10) sts across CO edge. Sl 4 (4, 5) sts pw to 7 sts on RH needle tip, leave rem 4 (4, 5) sts on dpn. **LG:** With E, K7. Turn. [11 (11, 12) sts for **RG** thumb; 7 sts for **LG** thumb]

Row 2 (24" needle): **LG:** K8. Using a dpn, PU 8 (8, 10) sts across CO edge. Sl 4 (4, 5) sts pw to 8 sts on RH needle tip, leave rem 4 (4, 5) sts on dpn. **RG:** Sl rem 4 (4, 5) sts from dpn to RH needle tip, knit to end. Turn. [12 (12, 13) sts per half]

Rnd 2:

Row 1: **RG:** K11 (11, 12). **LG:** Sl rem 4 (4, 5) sts from dpn to RH needle tip, knit across rem 7 sts. Turn. [11 (11, 12) sts per half]

Row 2: **LG:** K12 (12, 13) sts. Rep for **RG**. Turn.

[23 (23, 25) sts total per thumb]

Rnd 3:

Row 1: **RG:** K8 (8, 9), ssk, K1. **LG:** K1, K2tog, K8 (8, 9). Turn. [10 (10, 11) sts per half]

Row 2: **LG:** K9 (9, 10), ssk, K1. **RG:** K1, K2tog, K9 (9, 10). Turn. [11 (11, 12) sts per half]

Rnd 4: Knit.

Rnd 5:

Row 1: **RG:** K7 (7, 8), ssk, K1. **LG:** K1, K2tog, K7 (7, 8). Turn. [9 (9, 10) sts per half]

Row 2: **LG:** K8 (8, 9), ssk, K1. **RG:** K1, K2tog, K8 (8, 9). Turn. [10 (10, 11) sts per half]

Rnd 6: Knit. Do not cut E.

Rnd 7:

Row 1: **RG:** With G, K9 (9, 10). Rep for **LG**. Turn.

Row 2: **LG:** K7 (7, 8), ssk, K1. **RG:** K1, K2tog, K7 (7, 8). Turn. [9 (9, 10) sts per half]

Rnd 8: Knit.

Rnd 9:

All sts will be shifted slightly in this rnd to accommodate thumb hoodie setup.

Row 1: **RG:** K2 and sl on lockable marker, K7 (7, 8) sts. **LG:** K9 (9, 10) sts and sl last 2 sts from RH needle to lockable marker. Turn. [7 (7, 8) sts per half]

Row 2: LG: Sl 2 sts from marker to RH needle tip, K7 (7, 8), sl rem 2 sts to lockable marker. **RG:** K2 sts and sl to lockable marker, K7 (7, 8) sts, sl 2 sts from marker to LH needle then K2. Turn. Cut G. [9 (9, 10) sts per half]

[16 (16, 18) sts total per thumb]

Thumb Hoodie Setup

Rnd 1:

Row 1: RG: With E, K7 (7, 8), sl 2 sts from marker to LH needle, K2. **LG:** Sl 2 sts from marker to LH needle tip, K9 (9, 10). Turn. [9 (9, 10) sts per half]

Row 2: LG: *With E, knit into shoulder of st below as if to LIR but do not knit corresponding st on LH needle; instead sl it pw to RH needle; rep from * to end. Rep for **RG**. Turn. [18 (18, 20) sts per half]

Rnd 2:

Row 1: Knit. Turn.

Row 2: LG: Hold 2 dpn parallel to each other in right hand. Work across 24" needle, alternately slipping inc sts to back dpn and sl st to front dpn. Rep for **RG**. [9 (9, 10) sts per dpn]

Sl sts pw from front dpn to waste yarn. With 24" needle, knit across sts on back dpn. Rep for **RG**. Turn.

FINISH THUMB

Rnds 3–8: Beg with a purl row, work in garter st.

Rnd 9:

BO as for pinky. Cut E.

Thumb Hoodie

Setup

RG: With back of hand facing, sl 9 (9, 10) sts from waste yarn to 16" needle. With G, knit. Cont with same needle tip and using the backward loop cast on (page 11), CO 10 sts. Sl these 10 sts pw to 24" needle. Fold needles so both tips face to the left and open end of CO edge as well as working yarn face toward the cables. Follow instructions for "Setting Up the Needles" (page 20).

Sl thumbs behind needle cables; sts on 16" needle are attached to glove and sts on 24" needle are not.

LG: With back of hand facing and **RG** to right of needle tip, sl 9 (9, 10) sts from waste yarn to 16" needle. Both gloves sit on 16" needle.

Work across **RG** first by slipping all its sts from LH to RH needle. With G and same needle tip knit across all sts of **LG**. Cont with same needle tip and using the backward loop cast on, CO 10 sts. Sl these 10 sts pw to 24" needle. Fold needles so both tips face to the left and open end of CO edge as well as working yarn face toward the cables. Follow instructions for "Setting Up the Needles" (page 20).

Back of hand is facing, both needles are in front of glove; sts on 16" needle are attached to glove and sts on 24" needle are not. Turn. [19 (19, 20) sts per hoodie]

Rnd 1: Knit.

Rnds 2–7:

Row 1: Knit. Turn.

Row 2: LG: *K1, P1; rep from * to end. Rep for **RG**. Turn.

Rnds 8–14: Knit.

Large

Rnd 15: Knit.

Small and Medium

Rnd 15:

Rows 1 and 2: **RG:** K1, M1L, knit to end. Rep for **LG**. Turn. (10 sts per half) Cut G.

All Sizes

Rnd 1: With C, *(K3, K2tog); rep from * to end. (16 sts total per thumb)

Rnds 2 and 3: Knit.

Rnd 4: *(K2, K2tog); rep from * to end. (12 sts total per thumb)

Rnds 5 and 6: Knit.

Rnd 7: *(K1, K2tog); rep from * to end. (8 sts total per thumb)

Rnd 8: Knit.

Rnd 9: (K2tog) twice then BO rem sts. (2 sts total per thumb)

Rnd 10: RG: Sl st from 24" needle to dpn. Twist dpn so that st with working yarn is at needle tip, K1 from 16" needle. Both sts sit on dpn.

Using 2 dpns, work I-cord (page 14) for 1½". Cut yarn, leaving 6" tail, pull through to WS forming a button loop with I-cord, secure. Rep for **LG**.

Weave in ends.

MITTEN HOODIE
Setup

RG: With backs of hands facing, sl 28 (30, 32) sts from waste yarn to 16" needle. With A, knit, cont with same needle tip and using the backward loop cast on, CO 30 (30, 34) sts. Sl these 30 (30, 34) sts to 24" needle. Fold needles so both tips face to the left and open end of CO edge as well as working yarn face toward the cables. Follow instructions for "Setting Up the Needles" (page 20).

With back of hand facing, sl glove bodies behind both needle cables; sts on 16" needle are attached to glove and sts on 24" needle are not.

LG: With back of hand facing and **RG** to right of tip, sl 28 (30, 32) sts from waste yarn to 16" needle. Both gloves sit on 16" needle. Beg with **RG** and sl all sts from LH to RH needle. With A and same needle tip, knit across all sts of **LG**. Cont with same needle tip and using the backward loop cast on, CO 30 (30, 34) sts. Sl these 30 (30, 34) sts pw to 24" needle. Fold needles so both tips face to the left and open end of CO edge as well as working yarn face toward the cables. Follow instructions for "Setting Up the Needles."

Back of hand is facing, both needles are sitting in front of glove; sts on 16" needle are attached to glove and sts on 24" needle are not. Turn.

Small and Large

Rnds 1–7:

Row 1 (16" needle): With A, knit. Turn.

Row 2 (24" needle): **LG:** (K2, P2) to last 2 sts, K2. Rep for **RG**. Turn.

Medium

Rnds 1–6: Work as for Small and Large.

Rnd 7:

Row 1: **RG:** K10, (M1L, K10) twice. Rep for **LG**. Turn. (32 sts per half)

Row 2: **LG:** *(K2, P2); rep from * to end. Rep for **RG**. Turn.

All Sizes

[58 (62, 66) sts total for hoodie]

Rnd 8:

Row 1: **RG:** With A, *K3, with E, K1; rep from * to end. Rep for **LG**. Turn.

Row 2: **LG:** (With E, K2, with A, P2) to last 2 sts, with E, K2. Rep for **RG**. Turn.

Rnd 9:

Row 1: **RG:** With A, *K2, with E, K2; rep from * to end. Rep for **LG**. Turn.

Row 2: **LG:** (With E, K2, with A, P2) to last 2 sts, with E, K2. Rep for **RG**. Turn.

Rnd 10:

Row 1: **RG:** With A, K1, with E, K3; rep from * to end. Rep for **LG**. Turn.

Row 2: **LG:** (With E, K2, with A, P2) to last 2 sts, with E, K2. Rep for **RG**. Turn. Cut A.

Rnds 11–14:

Row 1: With E, knit. Turn.

Row 2: **LG:** *K2, P2; rep from * to last 2 sts, K2. Rep for **RG**. Turn. Cut E.

Rnds 15 and 16:

Row 1: With G, knit. Turn.

Row 2: **LG:** *K2, P2; rep from * to last 2 sts, K2. Rep for **RG**. Turn. Cut G.

Rnd 17: With D, knit. Cut D.

Rnds 18–21: With F, knit.

Small

Rnd 22 (inc rnd):

Row 1: **RG:** K2, M1L, knit to last st, M1L, K1. Rep for **LG**. (30 sts per half)

Row 2: Knit.

Medium

Rnd 22 (inc rnd):

Row 1: **RG:** K7, M1L, (K6, M1L) 3 times, K7. Rep for **LG.** (36 sts per half)

Row 2: **LG:** K5, M1L, (K4, M1L) 5 times, K5. Rep for **RG.** (36 sts per half)

Large

Rnd 22 (inc rnd):

Row 1: **RG:** K7, M1L, (K6, M1L) 3 times, K7. Rep for **LG.** (36 sts per half)

Row 2: **LG:** K8, M1L, K18, M1L, K8. Rep for **RG.** (36 sts per half)

All Sizes

[60 (72, 72) sts total per hoodie]

Rnds 23–32: Work chart C.

Rnd 33 (dec rnd):

Cont with B.

Small

Row 1: **RG:** K1, ssk, knit to last 3 sts, K2tog, K1. Rep for **LG.** (28 sts per half)

Row 2: **LG:** K1, ssk, knit to last 3 sts, K2tog, K1. Rep for **RG.** (28 sts per half)

Medium

Row 1: **RG:** (K4, ssk) 3 times, (K2tog, K4) 3 times. Rep for **LG.** (30 sts per half)

Row 2: **LG:** (K4, ssk) 3 times, (K2tog, K4) 3 times. Rep for **RG.** (30 sts per half)

Large

Row 1: **RG:** (K7, ssk) twice, (K2tog, K7) twice. Rep for **LG.** (32 sts per half)

Row 2: **LG:** (K7, ssk) twice, (K2tog, K7) twice. Rep for **RG.** (32 sts per half)

All Sizes

[56 (60, 64) sts total per hoodie]

Rnd 34: Knit.

Glove Hoodie Crown

Rnd 1: With B, *K2, K2tog; rep from * to end. [42 (45, 48) sts total per hoodie]

Rnd 2: Knit. Cut B.

Rnd 3: With G, knit.

Rnd 4: *K1, K2tog; rep from * to end. [28 (30, 32) sts total per hoodie]

Rnds 5 and 6: With G, knit.

Rnd 7: *K2tog; rep from * to end. [14 (15, 16) sts total per hoodie]

Rnd 8: Knit. Cut G.

Rnd 9: With D, knit.

Small and Medium

Rnd 10:

Row 1: **RG:** *K2tog; rep from * to last st and sl st to lockable marker. Rep for **LG.** Turn.

Row 2: **LG:** Sl st to LH needle and (K2tog) to end. Rep for **RG.** Turn. [7 (8) sts total per hoodie]

Large

Rnd 10: *K2tog; rep from * to end. (8 sts total per hoodie)

Rnd 11:

***Row 1:* RG:** K2tog once, K1 (0, 0), (K2tog) 0 (1, 1) time. Rep for **LG**. Turn.

Row 2: K2tog across. Turn. [4 sts total per hoodie]

Rnd 12: RG: Sl 2 sts from 24" needle to dpn. Twist dpn so that st with working yarn sits at needle tip, K2 from 16" needle. 4 sts sit on dpn.

Using 2 dpns, beg I-cord (page 14) and work for 2¾". Cut 6" tail, pull through to wrong side forming a button loop with I-cord, secure. Rep for **LG**.

Weave in ends. Sew buttons opposite loops.

Chart A

16" needle: Work sts 1–31 twice—once per glove.
24" needle: Work sts 32–60 twice—once per glove.

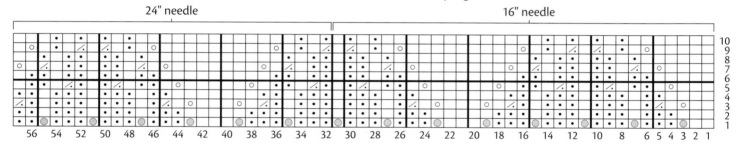

Key

☐	K
•	P
○	YO
╱	P2tog
◉	With A/B = MB; with C = MBB

Chart B

Work chart in rnds across both needles, all sts.
Small: Stitches 1–28
Medium: Stitches 1–30
Large: Stitches 1–32

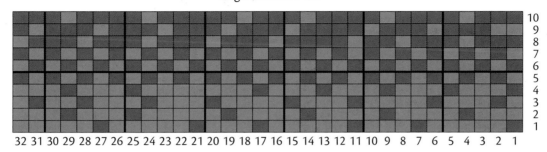

Key

■ Crabapple (F)
■ Teal (B)

Chart C

All sizes work chart across both needles, all sts.

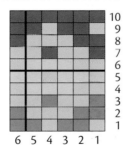

Key

□ Willow (A)
■ Teal (B)
□ Dusty Rose (D)
■ Crabapple Blossom (F)

abbreviations and glossary

[ ]	Work instructions within brackets as many times as directed
( )	Work instructions within parentheses in the place directed
*	Repeat instructions following
approx	approximately
beg	begin(ning)
BO	bind off
CC	contrasting color
cm	centimeter(s)
cn	cable needle(s)
CO	cast on
cont	continue(ing)(s)
dec	decrease(ing)(s)
dpn(s)	double-pointed needle(s)
g	gram(s)
inc	increase(ing)(s)
K	knit
K1B	knit in stitch below
K1f&b	knit into front and back of same stitch (see page 14)—1 stitch increased
K2tog	knit 2 stitches together (see page 12)—1 stitch decreased
kw	knitwise
LC	left cable
LG	left glove
LH	left hand
LIL	lifted increase left (page 13)
LIR	lifted increase right (page 13)
LM	left mitten
LPC	left purl cable
m	meter(s)
M1L	make 1 stitch left (see page 13)
M1R	make 1 stitch right (see page 13)

MC	main color
mm	millimeter(s)
oz	ounce(s)
P	purl
P2tog	purl 2 stitches together (see page 12)—1 stitch decreased
patt	pattern(s)
pm	place marker
psso	pass slipped stitch over
PU	pick up and knit
pw	purlwise
RC	right cable
rem	remain(ing)
rep(s)	repeat(s)
RG	right glove
RH	right hand
RM	right mitten
rnd(s)	round(s)
RPC	right purl cable
RS	right side
sl	slip
sl st(s)	slip stitch(es)—slip stitches purlwise unless instructed otherwise
ssk	slip 2 stitches knitwise, 1 at a time, to right needles, then insert left needle from left to right into front loops and knit 2 stitches together—1 stitch decreased (see page 12)
st(s)	stitch(es)
St st(s)	stockinette stitch(es)
tbl	through back loop(s)
tog	together
WS	wrong side
yd(s)	yard(s)
YO(s)	yarn over(s)

useful information

Yarn Weight Symbol and Category Names	Super Fine 1	Fine 2	Light 3	Medium 4	Bulky 5	Super Bulky 6
Type of Yarns in Category	Sock, Fingering, Baby	Sport, Baby	DK, Light Worsted	Worsted, Afghan, Aran	Chunky, Craft, Rug	Bulky, Roving
Knit Gauge Ranges in Stockinette Stitch to 4"	27 to 32 sts	23 to 26 sts	21 to 24 sts	16 to 20 sts	12 to 15 sts	6 to 11 sts
Recommended Needle in U.S. Size Range	1 to 3	3 to 5	5 to 7	7 to 9	9 to 11	11 and larger
Recommended Needle in Metric Size Range	2.25 to 3.25 mm	3.25 to 3.75 mm	3.75 to 4.5 mm	4.5 to 5.5 mm	5.5 to 8 mm	8 mm and larger

SKILL LEVELS

■□□□ **Beginner:** Projects for first-time knitters using basic knit and purl stitches. Minimal shaping.

■■□□ **Easy:** Projects using basic stitches, repetitive stitch patterns, and simple color changes. Simple shaping and finishing.

■■■□ **Intermediate:** Projects using a variety of stitches, such as basic cables and lace, simple intarsia, and techniques for double-pointed needles and knitting in the round. Midlevel shaping and finishing.

■■■■ **Experienced:** Projects using advanced techniques and stitches, such as short rows, Fair Isle, more intricate intarsia, cables, lace patterns, and numerous color changes.

METRIC CONVERSIONS

Yards x .91 = meters

Meters x 1.09 = yards

Grams x .0352 = ounces

Ounces x 28.35 = grams